"In *Filled to Be Emptied*, challenging, compelling, and ι case for understanding and p transformative faith that requiι Anyone who seeks to under world in which we live to look more like ... ... to labor without ceasing to cocreate a more just, inclusive world "on Earth as it is heaven"—should read this book."

—**ADAM RUSSELL TAYLOR**, president of Sojourners

"Jesus is the ultimate example of laying down his privilege for the sake of love and justice. Through this book, Robertson offers a thoughtful exploration of how we can follow in Jesus' footsteps. Robertson challenges each of us to confront our own privilege and choose the path that leads to flourishing for all."

—**JENNIFER BUTLER**, CEO of Faith in Public Life

"Robertson invites vulnerable self-reflection by his own example. Releasing ourselves from captive privilege and power to pursue peace and equity is uncomfortable. Yet ultimately, it is the path toward human flourishing. Read and be challenged to deeper levels of spiritual impact right here, right now."

—**CEDRIC HARMON**, executive director of Many Voices: A Black Church Movement for LGBT Justice

"Brandan Robertson has written a vigorous summons to the advantaged to heed the call of Christ. By an alert, sustained appeal to the ancient Christian hymn of Philippians 2, Robertson lines out how we who are advantaged may embrace an alternative life that resonates with God's good news. Though we may be 'filled' with the trinkets of capitalism, may we be 'emptied' of them in order to be 'filled' with the goodness of God. The focus is relentlessly on actual concrete practice. Robertson shows us a path that is emancipatory and reconciling—a major gift."

—**WALTER BRUEGGEMANN**, author of *Journey to the Common Good*

FILLED TO BE EMPTIED

FILLED TO BE EMPTIED

*The Path to Liberation
for Privileged People*

BRANDAN J. ROBERTSON

WESTMINSTER
JOHN KNOX PRESS
LOUISVILLE · KENTUCKY

First edition
Published by Westminster John Knox Press
Louisville, Kentucky

22 23 24 25 26 27 28 29 30 31—10 9 8 7 6 5 4 3 2 1

Book design by Drew Stevens
Cover design by Nita Ybarrra

Library of Congress Cataloging-in-Publication Data

Names: Robertson, Brandan, 1992- author.
Title: Filled to be emptied : the path to liberation for privileged people / Brandan J. Robertson.
Description: First edition. | Louisville, Kentucky : Westminster John Knox Press, [2022] | Includes bibliographical references. | Description based on print version record and CIP data provided by publisher.
Identifiers: LCCN 2021051546 (print) | LCCN 2021051547 (ebook) | ISBN 9780664267247 (paperback) | ISBN 9781646982325 (ebook)
Subjects: LCSH: Bible. Philippians, II, 5-11—Criticism, interpretation, etc. | Privilege (Social psychology) | Privilege (Social psychology)—Religious aspects. | Theology—Social aspects.
Classification: LCC HM671 (ebook) | LCC HM671 .R623 2022 (print) | DDC 305.5—dc23
LC record available at https://lccn.loc.gov/2021051546

Most Westminster John Knox Press books are available at special quantity discounts when purchased in bulk by corporations, organizations, and special-interest groups. For more information, please e-mail SpecialSales@wjkbooks.com.

If then there is any encouragement in Christ, any consolation from love, any sharing in the Spirit, any compassion and sympathy, make my joy complete: be of the same mind, having the same love, being in full accord and of one mind. Do nothing from selfish ambition or conceit, but in humility regard others as better than yourselves. Let each of you look not to your own interests, but to the interests of others. Let the same mind be in you that was in Christ Jesus,

> *who, though he was in the form of God,*
> *did not regard equality with God*
> *as something to be exploited,*
> *but emptied himself,*
> *taking the form of a slave,*
> *being born in human likeness.*
> *And being found in human form,*
> *he humbled himself*
> *and became obedient to the point of death—*
> *even death on a cross.*

> *Therefore God also highly exalted him*
> *and gave him the name*
> *that is above every name,*
> *so that at the name of Jesus*
> *every knee should bend,*
> *in heaven and on earth and under the earth,*
> *and every tongue should confess*
> *that Jesus Christ is Lord,*
> *to the glory of God the Father.*
> *—Philippians 2:1–11*

CONTENTS

Introduction

A PRIVILEGE PANDEMIC

In February 2020, I woke up in my hotel room in Geneva, Switzerland. I was coming to the end of a ten-day book tour across England and Switzerland and preparing for my last day of wandering through the ancient cobblestone streets, retracing the footsteps of John Calvin. As I turned on the television in my room, a breaking news alert came across the screen on the Swiss news channel. The subtitles read, "The First Case of Coronavirus Reported outside Geneva," and the camera immediately showed an interview with the husband and wife who had been the first known Swiss to contract the virus. "It's easier than a common cold!" the man with the virus scoffed. "I don't know why people are making such a big deal about this!" I laughed at the man's flippant attitude toward being ill and found myself at ease about the potential of this new virus that had been creating a buzz for the past few weeks. "Maybe it's not so bad after all," I thought.

Two weeks after I returned home to San Diego, I began to feel a bit under the weather. I posted to Facebook asking for advice from fellow San Diegans on how to fend off what I thought were bad allergies from the Santa Ana winds that often blow through our part of the world. A few days later, I had a high fever, body aches, and significant chest congestion. I called the doctor and was told that no testing was available, but that it was likely not the corona-virus. I should still, however, self-quarantine in bed until I felt better. So I did.

Two weeks after that, I had fully recovered and gone on with my life. At the beginning of the stay-at-home order, I was concerned that I might not be able to survive finan-cially. I had hard conversations with our church's book-keeper about potentially needing to lay off staff, skip pay periods, or take a cut to my already meager salary. But after a few weeks, it looked like things would be fine; I was spending less, saving more, and had secured some writ-ing projects that would give me extra money to save up for an emergency. So I continued living a fairly comfortable, albeit lonely, existence.

Eventually, I had an opportunity to take an antibody test to see if my body had, in fact, fought off COVID-19 when I was sick in March. The finger-prick test showed that I did have the antibodies, which likely meant that I had contracted the virus and fully recovered. Fortunately, none of my roommates caught the virus, nor any of the church staff with whom I had interacted early on in my sickness. I felt grateful to have survived what had now become a global pandemic ravaging countries around the world, and I hoped that I would now have some immunity, though there was not enough data to know that for sure.

Soon after, however, reports began to emerge that the virus was disproportionately affecting communities of color across the United States. Nearly every neighborhood of New York City that was primarily populated by commu-nities of color had a significantly higher percentage of hos-pitalizations and deaths than in white areas of the city. The reason for this disparity was simple: communities of color overwhelmingly have a lower average income and therefore fewer resources, plus many people in these communities were essential workers during the crisis, working in grocery stores, hospitals, restaurants, or pharmacies, where they could not maintain social distance. These communities were filled with folks who were risking their own health and well-being for the good of the broader population and were suffering the consequences.

As these trends continued and the data consistently confirmed these findings, I began to reflect on my own experience with COVID-19. Even though I had come to take the virus very seriously—advising my staff to stay home, practicing social distancing, and so on—the truth is that I too had a bit of a flippant attitude like that Swiss couple. I had not only survived the virus relatively unscathed, but I was actually doing pretty well during quarantine, getting healthier, being more productive, and enjoying more space to breathe and relax. I realized that for so many others even in my own neighborhood, which was primarily low income and 86 percent people of color, this pandemic was truly devastating.

How could it be that within the confines of my townhouse all was going so well for me, when right outside my door were thousands of neighbors whose lives had been completely upended by this pandemic? How could my church, which was neither large nor wealthy, be weathering the storm fairly well when the Spanish-speaking storefront church a block away, with twice as many members, was likely not going to survive this pandemic? How could we *still* have governmental systems and structures that favored people based on social class and ethnicity in the United States in 2020? This wasn't the first time I had wrestled with these questions, but in the middle of the pandemic, they hit me like a ton of bricks.

The thing is, these were not genuine questions. I knew the answer. Over the past decade I had much experience learning about the ways I participate in and benefit from the very thing behind the immense disparities in infection rates in communities of color. I had also experienced, in some small ways, just how ruthless and unfair this thing was when it finally was used against me when I came out as queer in 2016. This mysterious thing has risen to the top of our collective conversations, and talking about it makes many folks who benefit from it very nervous. The word for it is *privilege*.

This book is an exploration of the idea of privilege through the lens of the example set by a radical rabbi from Nazareth named Jesus. The goal of this book is to help those of us who identify as Jesus followers to begin a conversation about our own privilege and how we might utilize it as a tool to lead us into a more faithful obedience to the way of Jesus by working for the common good of our neighbors.

This call to repurpose privilege and power is nothing new—in fact, it's one of the earliest Christian practices. While the dialogue around privilege has only recently gained a new hearing in our culture, it was one of the major ways that the earliest followers of Jesus understood their role as disciples. One of the earliest Christian hymns, which the apostle Paul quotes in Philippians 2:5–11, describes how Jesus emptied himself of divine privilege. Exploring this hymn, verse by verse, will help us understand how Christ's example helps us to name, own, and repurpose our privilege and power for the good of others.

Conversations around the topic of privilege are often avoided because they can become deeply personal and are often eye-opening in ways that make us uncomfortable. But in this moment of human history, it is imperative for

Christians not to run from these conversations but rather lean into them all the more. The Spirit of God is stirring up a reformation within our day, exposing systems of oppression that have long been hidden, and calling us all to new ways of seeing and being in the world. This book is intended to help guide us through a process of understanding the current conversation around privilege and then empowering us to do something about it as individuals and as communities of faith. It's written by someone who has himself continually wrestled with these concepts over the past five years, and still has so much to learn and to reckon with in his own journey. I am not an expert on these issues, but I don't believe any of us need to be. Instead, we need to begin the conversations and do the work, which is precisely what this book is intended to do. So I hope that you will join with me on this journey of self-reflection, spiritual practice, and contemplative action that helps bring about a more just and equal world for absolutely everyone.

Chapter 1

THE PROBLEM OF PRIVILEGE

What are we talking about when we talk about privilege? We often hear this word thrown around in conversations related to racism and sexism in particular, but oftentimes many of us do not have a clue what exactly a person means when they use the term. Many of the people who are often described as privileged do not consciously feel the benefits that they are accused of possessing. In a different time, to be described as being privileged was a good thing, wasn't it? It's clear that for so many of us the conversation around privilege is anything but clear. And yet this conversation isn't going to end anytime soon—nor should it. So it is imperative for all people—especially those with privilege—to do the work to understand exactly what this word means for us and why using privilege properly is so vital, as I will claim, to living out the way of Jesus in our world today.

I was raised in a lower-middle- to lower-class community outside of Baltimore, Maryland, yet within one of the wealthiest counties in the country at the time. The disparities of wealth, status, and class were apparent to me every time I went to school. Many of my peers were decked out in name-brand clothing; they always had money to afford lunch at school, or even more enviably, money to have a car and be able to leave school and buy lunch at a nearby fast-food restaurant. Many of my peers could afford special trips, supplies, and opportunities that were offered by our incredible public school system. Many of my peers would go home to large houses every day and would take long family vacations to Mexico or Hawaii in the summer. My experience, on the other hand, was very different, and I was consciously aware of this difference.

I lived in an old mobile home in a large trailer park tucked away, out of sight, from the beautiful homes that surrounded us. My mother worked hard, at times working a part-time job at a retail store in addition to her full-time job at a doctor's office just to get by. My father worked sometimes, but his addiction to alcohol quickly began to prevent him from being very effective at making any substantial amount of money to support our family. My parents would struggle week by week to keep the bills paid and our family fed, and then to fund whatever other needs might arise. Because of this environment, there wasn't a huge emphasis on studying hard or excelling in school—my parents had much more pressing things to focus on, like our basic survival. So I was generally a straight C student throughout most of my education, and in middle and high school was doing very poorly in the areas of reading, writing, and math, which severely limited my ability to get into any reputable college. I also never really learned to drive beyond my initial learner's permit because I knew we could never afford a car for me, or even the driving-school classes that were required by law.

So when someone first spoke to me about my privilege, it was difficult for me to understand what they were talking about. Yes, it is true that I am a white man. But most of my peers growing up were *not* white—in fact, all my best friends throughout childhood were people of color—and all of them were significantly more well-off than my family was. How could my whiteness be such a source of privilege when it doesn't seem to have benefited my family all that much in my upbringing?

This is often the first way many respond when they first have their privilege called out, and at some level, it is valid. It's true that possessing a particular identity *alone* is not enough to guarantee that someone's life will necessarily be better off than others. Being white, or male, or straight, doesn't mean that you and your family will not face hardships, struggle, and even discrimination. Yet often in the dialogue around privilege, this truth is not given a fair hearing. Many sociologists say that this is one of the reasons why the world witnessed such disruptive political upheavals from 2016 through 2020. Much of the political dialogue had rightfully shifted to justice and equity for those who had traditionally been marginalized—people of color, women, LGBTQ+ individuals—but in that necessary shift, many politicians all but ignored the real, significant struggles of those who were not in those marginalized categories, which led to a political upheaval rooted in their sense of real desperation.

From this perspective, one might ask if the conversation around privilege is even appropriate at all. From the foundation of my upbringing, it'd be hard to make a case that my whiteness or my maleness benefited me in any meaningful way, right? If privilege means that possessing certain basic identities *always* confers a series of benefits, then I think we could say that claims of privilege are patently false. But what if the idea of privilege is getting at something more nuanced and complex?

The truth is that my upbringing was very difficult, and my parents still struggle to this day to rise above the socioeconomic reality we experienced as I was growing up.

My upbringing did cost me some significant opportunities and experiences that many of my peers had. Yet here in your hand you hold my sixth published book. At the time of this writing, I am a semester away from receiving my second master's degree. I am living in Southern California and my current income has placed me securely in the middle-class category; my starting salary at my job is about the same as my mother's salary after nearly twenty years in her job. Clearly, my upbringing didn't affect my attainment of "success" very much. I am doing fairly well, I'd say, despite all of the cards I was dealt growing up.

Some of my "success" may be attributed to my personality or personal fortitude (though I assure you, I am no beacon of psychological strength!), but the truth is that it seems quite obvious that there must have been *something* else at work to help me rise this far above the circumstances of my birth. Something seems to have been working in my favor to assist me in overcoming the multitude of hurdles that I faced. At least part of my own personal success can rightly be attributed to the concept of privilege.

DEFINING PRIVILEGE

Merriam-Webster's Dictionary defines "privilege" as "a right or immunity granted as a peculiar benefit, advantage, or favor."[1] In other words, it's some form of advantage given to a particular group of people that is not extended to others. In school, I remember being rewarded for good behavior by being allowed to choose from a series of "privileges," such as sitting at the teacher's desk for the day or not having to do a homework assignment. The teacher would always remind us as we redeemed our privilege that our reward was not our *right* and if we started slacking while enjoying it, it could and would be revoked. This picture helps us to understand privilege at its most basic: it's something we don't necessarily deserve but is extended to us as a favor. It's not a permanent reality, but when it is being enjoyed, it does come with a very real sense of advantage over others who do not enjoy the same benefit.

The definition of social privilege differs slightly. Scholar Justin D. García defines this kind of privilege as "certain social advantages, benefits, or degrees of prestige and respect that an individual has by virtue of belonging to certain social identity groups."[2] In this sense, one could approximately equate social privilege to being a member of a country club. If you have membership, you get access to the pools, the spa, the fine dining, and the golf green. But if you do not have membership, you will be promptly stopped at the gate and denied entry. Your lack of membership excludes you from this wide array of special amenities (i.e., benefits). The difference on the social side is that most of the time, these "memberships" are granted by nature of birth, are often unconscious to the ones who hold them, and therefore aren't acknowledged as privileges. They are not easily lost, and they are almost impossible to extend to others who are not born members of this privileged club.

To carry the metaphor a bit further, if you grow up in the confines of the country club, you may never realize that there is a world outside of the gates that is *significantly* different from the world you experience. If you are conditioned to believe that you *deserve* to go to college, to pursue a career of your dreams, to make a living wage, or to have even more rudimentary realities such as the right to vote or the right to *live freely*, then it is entirely possible that you may never realize that others cannot take these possibilities for granted, let alone have a reasonable hope of actually attaining them. In fact, it is one of the express jobs of those who operate the country club to block out the crasser realities of the world outside its walls specifically so those within the club do not have their conscience disturbed by the great disparities that exist just beyond the walls.

The truth is, if you live in North America, Great Britain, or much of Europe, you live in a society that was created by and intended for white, heterosexual, Christian men, and most of these societies were built with a very conscious belief that such people are *superior* to other kinds of humans, which allowed the colonizing founders of the modern Western world to marginalize, oppress, enslave, and kill all of the people who didn't look, love, and believe as they did. In America, for instance, the most revered foundational documents that established the nation codified the superiority of white, heterosexual, Christian men, and the inferiority of nonwhites, women, non-Christians, and by inference nonheterosexuals. Today, many of us have been taught to shrug off the words in the Declaration of Independence that refer to the indigenous peoples of the Americas as "Indian Savages" as simply antiquated language, as if those two words did not represent the prevailing mindset that has endured throughout the history of the United States and has continually allowed us to treat indigenous people as less human than white people.

The privileging of certain people was intentionally built into the bedrock of our society. The architects of our society knew what they were doing, and it was justified by deeply held beliefs, many rooted in Christianity, that fueled their hope to create a world where they lived as demigods over the land. Which brings us back to my upbringing. The primary reason that I was able to rise above the circumstances of my upbringing is because the society was set up to give me, as a white man, every opportunity to succeed. Study after study has shown that my poor grades likely posed less of a threat to my ability to get into college than they would have for a person of color. When I walk into a room for an interview at a school or a job, most of the people in that room have been subconsciously conditioned to believe that I am more capable and deserving, despite my flaws, than a person of color or a woman. Even though I grew up relatively poor, my skin color and my accent enable me to easily pass as wealthy, which gains me access and acceptance into social circles of those who truly are wealthy and powerful. I also get the chance to be bolder in my pursuit of things that I want because I live in a society where that's what white men are *supposed* to do, whereas women and people of color are not permitted to act in similar ways.

These are not small benefits. They are also not easily recognizable to those of us who are white men, but I guarantee that any person of color or non-male-identified person who reads the paragraph above would nod in agreement and be able to point out *many more* areas where society privileges my whiteness and my maleness that I have not even thought to mention. Remember, it's hard to see the reality of one's benefits if you've never taken time to wander beyond the marble walls of the country club.

IMPLICIT BIAS

Hopefully the examples above have helped to clarify what exactly is meant when we talk about privilege in the social context. The natural next question for those who possess such privilege is "Now what do I do?" No one chose to be born with any of the core identities that we possess, nor is it fundamentally wrong to have privilege. At the most basic level, privilege is morally neutral. Receiving an unearned benefit or advantage is usually viewed as a good thing, and no matter what identities one possesses, it would seem foolish to reject such a blessing. One should certainly not feel bad for receiving such a gift. Where privilege crosses firmly into immorality is when the advantage comes at an unfair cost to others, to put it mildly. And when it comes to the privilege of white, heterosexual, Christian men, the cost to everyone else has been astronomical.

To use myself as an example once again, if my college admittance had been based solely on merit, my straight C average in high school would surely have limited my ability to get into *most* of the private colleges and universities that I applied to. Numerous studies have shown that if a Black student (or anyone with a "Black-sounding" name) had submitted the exact same transcripts with their application, they would have been *far* less likely to be admitted to a school than I would be.[3] I don't think that most college admissions teams are consciously seeking to be racist in their decisions (though some certainly are), but in a society where whiteness has been set as the ideal in nearly every aspect of the culture, the subconscious assumption is that white people must be smarter or more capable of academic improvement than people of color.

This unconscious discriminatory attitude is known as *implicit bias* or *implicit social cognition* and is well documented by social scientists and psychologists. The Kirwan Institute at Ohio State University defines implicit bias as "the attitudes or stereotypes that affect our understanding, actions, and decisions in an unconscious manner. Activated involuntarily, without awareness or intentional control."[4] When it is defined this way, it becomes easy to see that implicit bias exists in every person, in every culture, in every era. It emerges from our cultural conditioning, which includes the media we consume, the religion we practice, the family we come from, the neighborhood we grow up in, the politicians who represent us, the laws we're held accountable to—just about every aspect of our daily lives. These biases are all pervasive and automatic, and they don't often reflect what we consciously believe or the ideals we confess to be true for us.

Because implicit bias exists unconsciously within us, if we are to ever address and change them, we must be careful to identify exactly *what* the dominant biases in our culture are, become aware of them in our own actions and thinking, and then actively work against them. This is precisely why conversations around racism have recently shifted from being about resisting racism to being *antiracist*,[5] suggesting that to actually kill the disease of racism in our culture, we must not simply believe that racism is wrong, but we must actively work to oppose racist thinking and action in our own consciousness and in society at large.

If we don't understand the power of implicit bias, then we may never realize just how pervasive and dangerous our exploitation of social privilege is. I remember lecturing to a primarily white audience at the University of Calgary in Canada on the power of implicit bias. During the talk, I made a statement along the lines of "all of us are racist, and we must work to root out racism within us." Immediately, a white man spoke up and said, "I am not a racist, and I refuse to accept that all of us are racist." His reactionary response is understandable if we don't consider the reality of implicit bias. That man probably did work quite hard to not be racist in his speech, in his actions, and in his decision making, as all morally responsible people should. But *not being racist* in our actions is not the same as *not having racist biases and impulses* in our subconscious minds. Surely it is unlikely that any white person who has been raised in a society with historic race inequities like the United States and Canada will not have the residue of racism covering their subconscious mind. But unless we take time for honest self-reflection and open conversation with those who experience the world differently than we do, we may very likely not realize the extent to which we are infected with implicit biases.

Our privilege is one of the primary blinders to our implicit bias. If we don't have to think about how others' biases might impact our well-being in our day-to-day lives, it is likely that we possess some level of privilege. And if we do possess privilege, it is likely that we are unaware of the way that we naturally and subconsciously assign value to others who are like us and have an aversion to those who are different. Which is why all of us who seek to be agents of justice in society, and especially those of us who espouse the values of Jesus Christ, must commit ourselves to engage in conscious reflection on our privilege and bias, and then work not just to suppress it within ourselves and society, but also to actively train our minds to think and react differently and work to ensure the systems and structures of society do the same.

THAT THE BLIND MAY SEE

But how can Christianity help us with our privilege and bias? How can we as followers of Christ begin to work to understand and address these realities? One of the central goals of Jesus in the Gospel accounts is to help "the blind receive their sight" (Matt. 11:5, NIV). Throughout the Gospel accounts, we see many stories of Jesus literally healing those who are physically blind, but it seems upon closer reading that his central concern was not primarily physical but spiritual blindness. In fact, when Jesus is speaking about salvation to a Jewish leader named Nicodemus, he says, "Very truly I tell you, no one can see the kingdom of God unless they are born again." (John 3:3 NIV). The idea Jesus is communicating is that humans have a *vision* problem. We cannot *see* what is true and real, we cannot perceive the reality of God's kingdom emerging around us in the present moment. Similarly, if we cannot perceive what God's desires are for the world, then we will not know just how far off the mark we are from those desires.

The way of Jesus is meant to help us gradually begin to receive our sight, and the more we see, the more we are called to repentance, which literally means "to change direction," to begin walking on a new path toward a different reality. This seeing comes to us only by allowing the Spirit of God to work within us to convict and compel us to follow the way of Jesus. We're told time and time again that this path is not an easy one and that it will cost us greatly.

Those of us who call ourselves Christians have an obligation to heed the call of the gospel to work with God to bring renewal and redemption to the world. At the very heart of our faith stands the example of Jesus, which we are called to follow in this profound command of the apostle Paul: "Do nothing out of selfish ambition or vain conceit. Rather, in humility value others above yourselves" (Phil. 2:3 NIV). Selfishness, vanity, and pride are antithetical to what it means to follow Jesus, and yet social privilege and bias exist for the purpose of seeking our own benefit, help privileged individuals to appear as the ideal, and are rooted in an obscene (if subconscious) sense of pride in one's identities as superior to others. If we take the call of Jesus seriously, then it is imperative that we begin the hard work of self-assessment to discover our own implicit biases and areas in which we have been granted unearned privilege in ways that negatively impact those who are not like us.

This self-examination and reckoning with our own exploitation of privilege and our implicit bias isn't only for the good of others, however. The subversive promise of Jesus is that when we are willing to give up our pursuit of our own benefit for the sake of others, that is when we truly receive the fulfillment that we're all longing for. Working to be antiracist, antisexist, antihomophobic, antitransphobic, antixenophobic not only benefits the communities that have been historically harmed by our pursuit of such advantage, but it benefits the privileged as well.

When we begin to create a society where true equity is our chief aim, where our care for our neighbor drives us to selfless action on their behalf, when we seek to give more than we seek to store up for ourselves, that way of being will reap blessings in our soul and in our daily living. A more just and equitable society emerges, where we all are cared for and have access to the resources we need to thrive. We will even tap into the greatest blessing of all—that deep sense of knowing that we are being used as channels of God's light and healing in the world, which at once fulfills our deepest longing and spurs us on to more service, more work, and more solidarity with marginalized communities. What could be more Christlike than that?

DISCUSSION QUESTIONS

1. What aspects of your identity bestow unearned privilege on you? What does the privilege you have look like in your day-to-day life?
2. Why do you think conversations about privilege can make us so uncomfortable?
3. What people in your sphere of influence are potentially disadvantaged because of your privilege?
4. When was the first time you had a conversation about privilege? What was that experience like for you?
5. How do you respond to the author's statement that "all of us are racist, and we must work to root out racism within us"? Can you identify areas of implicit bias within yourself?
6. How does your faith inform the way you think about privilege? What steps might God be asking you to take to potentially pave the way for true reform and renewal?

Chapter 2
PARADOXOLOGY

I have long had a fascination with the practices and beliefs of the early Christians, primarily because their religion was so dramatically different from much of what has become known as Christianity in the modern world. Rather than being primarily a community of worship, the earliest Christians looked more like a radical sociopolitical movement with religious undertones. As biblical scholar Richard Horsley notes, "Jesus launched a mission of social renewal among subject peoples."[1] Scholar Obery Hendricks echoes, "In short, the followers of the risen Jesus did not just proclaim a new reality, they lived it. It was this, the power of the testimony of their lives and the demonstrated strength of their convictions, that laid the basis for the faith of millions and modeled a new way of being human that has since transformed the world."[2]

The early Christians lived out a new way of being, not just for their personal lives, but for society at large. Their movement was profoundly powerful precisely because it wasn't simply a new religious path that emerged, but a practical new way to begin reordering one's life in hopes of renewing society as a whole.

For further proof that the early Christians were primarily concerned with a new way of living that challenged the political and social ordering of their society, one needn't look any further than one of the earliest hymns, recorded in a letter of the apostle Paul written to the church at Philippi, Greece, a church that Paul himself founded. In Philippians 2, the apostle quotes what has become known as the Kenosis Hymn because of the use of the unique Greek term *ekenōsen*, meaning "to empty," to describe Christ's behavior and posture as he ministered. This is my translation of Philippians 2:5–11, in which Paul quotes the hymn:

> Have the same way of thinking within you that was also within Christ Jesus:
>
>> Who existed in the form of God
>> and was equal with God,
>>> yet did not consider that his equality with
>>> God was something that should be seized
>>> for his own benefit.
>> But he emptied himself,
>>> taking on the role of the slave, born in human
>>> form.
>> Being found in human form he humbled himself
>> by becoming obedient as far as death,
>>> even the worst kind of death—
>>> death that comes through a cross.
>> For this reason, God has greatly exalted him
>>> and gave him the name
>>> that is above every other name,
>> so that at the name of Jesus,
>> every knee will bend—
>> of all beings in the universe—
>> and every tongue will gladly confess that Jesus
>> Christ is Lord, to the glory of God the Father.

Modern scholarship has raised questions about whether these words, quoted by Paul, were in fact a hymn that was sung or a creed that was recited, but either way, it seems clear that these words were important to the early Christian movement. While much ink has been spilt to describe and take apart the *theology* of these verses, it is more appropriate to consider the directives that this hymn prescribes. After all, Paul prefaces his recitation of the hymn with a command, "Have the same way of thinking within you that was also within Christ Jesus" (v. 5). These words were less a theological formula and more an articulation of the mindset, worldview, and actions of Jesus, and those who claim to be a part of his movement are invited to adopt this same mindset as a way of living.

This hymn is one of the clearest indicators of just how radical the early followers of Jesus were. These are not mere religious platitudes or dogmatic statements to be proclaimed as truth—they outline the very attitude of Jesus, the mindset that fueled his courageous proclamation of an alternative kingdom to Caesar's, which ultimately cost him his life. The early church, following Jesus, sought to form new families, new communities, and new societies, not through seeking to overthrow the empire from the top down, but through slowly, subversively, creating the ideal world that Jesus spoke of from the ground up. They embodied the best of what might be called in modern vernacular "socialism" in their communities—functioning as communes where people brought their resources together and redistributed them so that everyone was provided for. This new miniature society within a society was obviously very attractive, especially to the marginalized and disadvantaged, and thousands of people would join the burgeoning Jesus movement within the first few decades of its founding.

And its appeal, I suggest, was the formula for living found in this ancient hymn. The Kenosis Hymn represents what I think is best called a "paradoxology"—an amalgam of *paradox,* roughly meaning "mysterious, seemingly contradictory truth," and *doxology,* meaning "song of praise." Jesus' entire social and religious vision was paradoxical compared to the common understanding of how to create substantive change in the world, both in his time and in ours. It is this subversive paradox that results in the "doxology," the worship of Christ by Christians because we become captivated by the true power and beauty in Jesus' path—one that has been proclaimed repeatedly throughout history yet continues to be ignored or disbelieved by each generation.

After all, how could emptying oneself of power and privilege ultimately help one establish a new kingdom? How could willingly taking on the form of a slave, the lowest caste of the Greco-Roman social ladder in the first century, lead to one's exaltation? How could willingly dying the death of the worst kind of criminal result in God bestowing the title of ultimate power—"Lord"—on anyone? None of that, in terms of worldly power, seems to make any sense. This paradoxology is the subversive power of Christianity, and it is the very reason why Paul writes in 1 Corinthians 1:18 that Jesus' path is "foolishness to those who are perishing, but to us who are being saved it is the power of God."

Humans have always been hell-bent on pursuing power by force, storing up wealth for ourselves while others suffer, and believing that satisfaction can be found only through domination. This path does in fact lead to "perishing"—we've seen it time and time and time again. And the path of nonviolent resistance, of leveraging one's own

privilege to benefit others, of becoming a servant to the
world, seems to defy logic. It feels like a losing strategy. I
remember listening to then Senator Barack Obama declare
as much in a speech at Sojourners' Call to Renewal Con-
ference at National City Christian Church in Washington,
DC, in 2006. In that speech, he said:

> Which passages of Scripture should guide our public
> policy? Should we go with Leviticus, which suggests
> slavery is ok and that eating shellfish is abomination?
> How about Deuteronomy, which suggests stoning
> your child if he strays from the faith? Or should we
> just stick to the Sermon on the Mount—a passage that
> is so radical that it's doubtful that our own Defense
> Department would survive its application?[3]

Obama was speaking in the context of the need for the separation of church and state, but in doing so, he highlighted
the very reason that Jesus' path is so radical. He's right—the
American Defense Department *couldn't* survive the application of the Sermon on the Mount. Jesus not only taught
but demonstrated that it's only through giving up the pursuit of power and privilege, which is the very thing that the
Defense Department is charged with defending, that true
and lasting change becomes possible.

Now, I am not suggesting that the American government, or any government, should necessarily seek to
embody the way of Jesus. Again, Jesus never tried to convert the power structures of his day, but rather worked
within them to convert individuals to a new way of seeing and being. Modern governments have a practical role,
to mitigate against human depravity and violence and to

organize their society in a way that seeks the flourishing of their citizens. Nonetheless, the point still stands. The reason that *no government* has *ever* tried to take the teachings of Jesus seriously is precisely because they *require* utilizing power for the good of *other nations,* including enemies. There is absolutely no room for nationalism or an "America First" policy in Jesus' teaching.

CHRISTLESS CHRISTIANITY

It's not just governments that find Jesus' teachings all but impossible to embrace. Most Christians throughout history have refused to buy into Jesus' way of seeing and being. Jesus himself knew that this would be the case; it is precisely why he said, "Enter through the narrow gate; for the gate is wide and the road is easy that leads to destruction, and there are many who take it. For the gate is narrow and the road is hard that leads to life, and there are few who find it" (Matt. 7:13–14). A rare remnant of Christians throughout history have taken Jesus' words seriously and conformed their lives to them—even in Scripture, this sort of radical emulation of Christ is surprisingly rare. Thankfully, the New Testament makes it clear that this path is one that takes time to embody, a lifetime of striving to conform our lives ever so gradually to the image of Christ. This is the promise and power of grace.

The problem is that many people who call themselves Christians don't even *try* to follow the path of Christ. In fact, throughout history, pastors and theologians have intentionally constructed theologies that get Christians off the hook of seeking to model Jesus' examples. For instance, Pastor Tullian Tchividjian, a grandson of evangelist Billy

Graham, wrote about Jesus' teachings in the Sermon on the Mount:

> In the Sermon on the Mount, Jesus wants to set us free by showing us our need for a rightness we can never attain on our own—an impossible righteousness that's always out of our reach. The purpose of the Sermon on the Mount is to demolish all notions that we can reach the righteousness required by God—it's about exterminating all attempts at self-sufficient moral endeavor. So, in the deepest sense, the Sermon on the Mount is not a goal, but a wall we crash into so that we finally cry out "I can't do it!"[4]

On one hand, I can agree that it is all but impossible to fully obey the teachings and example of Christ. We will never truly and fully love all of our enemies, sell all of our possessions to give to the poor, or resist the urge to objectify others. But to simply throw our hands up and say, "I can't do it!" and then claim that we can never reach the righteousness required by God seems to miss the point completely.

The gospel of Jesus *is* about striving to become more like Christ. The commands of Jesus *are* about working with God to bring about renewal and redemption to the world. The Christian life is *not* meant to be a continual basking in the grace of God, waiting for the Holy Spirit to do some magical work within us to make us more righteous. No, it's about a commitment to continue to strive to make Jesus' vision of our lives and the world a reality in our sphere of influence. It is true that you cannot follow Jesus *perfectly,* and yet his invitation to never stop trying remains.

This is the difference between a Christianity that is primarily rooted in theology and one that is primarily rooted in practice. Again, there is a good reason that nowhere in the New Testament are we given a systematic theology or doctrinal statement—that was never the primary goal. We are told repeatedly, however, how we are to organize ourselves and how to practically live out the subversive, sacrificial way of Jesus in our day-to-day lives. This is the true worship that God has always desired, as beautifully stated by the apostle James, the brother of Jesus, who said, "Religion that God our Father accepts as pure and faultless is this: to look after orphans and widows in their distress and to keep oneself from being polluted by the world" (Jas. 1:27 NIV). It's a religion of compassionate action and a religion of resistance to the wisdom and ways of the systems of this world.

In the same way that Paul used the Kenosis Hymn to teach the church at Philippi how to think and live in a Christlike way, we would also be well served to utilize it as our path for living a life that reflects the values of Jesus. Whether we as individuals have a great deal of privilege or little to none, the kenotic way of Jesus offers us a path toward collective liberation, spiritual maturity, and healing for all of creation.

A POWER STRUGGLE

In the early church, there was a significant division between disciples who followed the apostles James and Peter and those who followed the apostle Paul.[5] If you read the entirety of the New Testament with this division in mind, you begin to see signs of it everywhere. One of the clearest descriptions of this division is in Paul's Letter to the Galatians:

When [Peter] came to Antioch, I opposed him to his face, because he stood condemned. For before certain men came from James, he used to eat with the Gentiles. But when they arrived, he began to draw back and separate himself from the Gentiles because he was afraid of those who belonged to the circumcision group. (Gal. 2:11–12 NIV)

This dispute exposes two fundamental differences between the kinds of faith that the two groups represented. Peter and James knew Jesus, walked with Jesus, and were commissioned by Jesus to carry forward the mantle of the movement he started. They believed that Jesus desired two things from his followers: first, to remain committed to their Jewish faith with all its practices and traditions, and second, to build the kingdom of God on earth as it is in heaven through subversive acts of charity—often called "good works."

As far as we know, Paul never met Jesus. In fact, he had been one of the leading opposers of the Jesus movement, responsible for the murder of many Christians. After he had a vision of Jesus on the road to persecute more Christians in Damascus, he began to call himself an apostle and proclaimed a different version of Christian faith: one that does away with almost everything Jewish about the way of Jesus so that it would be more appealing to Gentiles, and focuses more on the importance of believing things about who Jesus was and receiving a divine gift through such belief.

From an outsider's perspective, it is logical to conclude that Peter and James's version of Christianity most accurately represented what Jesus taught and expected from his disciples. Paul, after his miraculous conversion, sought to see the movement expand more rapidly and so made several innovative changes—some helpful and some troubling—that allowed it to do just that, which is precisely what we see in Galatians. Peter and James didn't want to fraternize with Gentiles or eat their food, because that violated kosher laws. But Paul wanted the divisions between Jews and Gentiles to be removed and wanted to make it easier for Gentiles to believe in Christ, so he opposed what he saw as exclusivism in Peter and James's theology, which required any new converts to obey Jewish laws *and* get circumcised, which obviously would deter almost any male Gentile from joining the Jesus movement.

In one sense, Paul can be seen as the apostle of inclusion, the one who made Christ's message more accessible to the world and the sole reason for Christianity's rapid growth and spread around the world. But on the other hand, we have good reason to be skeptical of Paul's version of the teachings of Jesus because, again, he never actually met him. This point is important because the Christianity of James and Peter was *primarily* concerned with doing justice, living humbly, and serving one's neighbor. It didn't seek to convert people to a new religion—in fact, it encouraged Jewish folks to stay a part of their own religious tradition—but urged them to adopt a way of living that brought about the kingdom of God that Jesus proclaimed.

Read the Letter of James in the New Testament, and you will see how the brother of Jesus understands the gospel: it is primarily about faith that *works*. The entire text is practical and hands-on, requiring disciples to engage in a new way of living more so than believing new doctrines and dogmas. The writings of Paul, on the other hand, skew much more theological. While I won't deny that Paul does have some beautiful passages about how Christians should actively live out our faith, much of his writing seeks to offer a theology of Jesus that most of the earliest Christians don't seem to have believed, at least initially. For the early disciples, following "the Way" was about creating a new social order from the ground up (see Acts 2:42–47) while remaining Jewish, rather than adopting an entirely new religion and worldview.

Which is why the Philippians letter and the inclusion of the Kenosis Hymn is so important. Most scholars believe that the book of Philippians isn't one letter, but rather multiple texts and teachings merged into one document.[6] Philippians is one of Paul's earlier collections of teachings, composed around AD 55, and it reflects a great deal of practical instruction on how to live as a community (the type of instruction one would expect from James and Peter), as well as some of Paul's own theological innovations.

The Kenosis Hymn itself is a unique text because it is almost universally agreed to be an earlier Christian hymn, not authored by Paul, and thus it contains the more "active" understanding of who Jesus was and what his mission was in the world. The text of the hymn says nothing about salvation or resurrection—two of Paul's most important recurring topics—which suggests that it is a true reflection of how the early Christians believed and lived. Theirs was a faith based on imitating Jesus, who they believed was God in the flesh, yet who showed us that we absolutely *could* live the life that God intended for us to live as mere humans. They believed that Christ emptied himself of his divine nature, and therefore he became truly human, and everything he does is in human strength.

In this sense, the hymn truly is a challenge, a pattern, and a prescription for disciples of Christ. The fact that Paul precedes the hymn with a command to adopt this as a way of operating is a clear indicator that it was expected that followers of Jesus could and *should* seek to live in the pattern of Jesus' own life. A faith that is not embodied in *active engagement in the healing of the world* is not a Christ-rooted faith at all.

IS SACRIFICE REASONABLE?

Recent scholarship has raised an apt concern around the language of kenosis and how it has been used historically to abuse and oppress minorities and women.[7] Is it reasonable or just to tell someone who lives in a society that marginalizes and oppresses them to sacrifice themselves for the good of others? Is it fair to declare that God desires those who have been stripped of dignity and equity to empty themselves and to take on the form of a slave to please God? These are not easy questions to contemplate because the answer is not at all clear in a biblical sense. Instead, much nuance is required to engage this concern.

On the most basic level, I do believe that following Jesus is a call to sacrifice ego, privilege, and power, giving it up to be of benefit to the collective renewal of the world. I cannot see any way around such a call in the New Testament. But it also must be noted that Jesus was primarily concerned with *empowering* the oppressed, not emptying them of their strength. He declared that in his kingdom, "the last will be first" (Matt. 20:16), a statement that must have caused the privileged and powerful who heard him speak those words to shudder. Jesus described a world where the power structures were turned upside down, a revolutionary reality where the poor, the marginalized, the oppressed, the despised, the excluded were given the place of authority over the world. He didn't describe simply a leveling of the playing field, but a fundamental restructuring of the social hierarchy.

I believe that Jesus did this precisely because he knew that those who had been abused, rejected, exploited, and cast aside knew more deeply than anyone how inadequate and evil the human systems of power fundamentally are. When oppressed people are given the power, they do not easily fall into the same traps as the privileged people do, because they know what it's like to be on the receiving end of the evils of oppressive structures. Jesus seems to trust that when the "least of these" gain power, they will not act retributively, but are perhaps the only ones who will know how to bring restoration to the world, and *even* to their former oppressors. In Jesus' ordering of the world, the marginalized are empowered precisely because of the wisdom and insight they have that has been disregarded by the powerful.

So when we're applying the paradigm of the Kenosis Hymn to the Christian life of a marginalized or oppressed person, we must be careful not to suggest that its directives somehow suggest that God desires them to empty themselves of their identities or their own pursuit of equity and justice, but rather, to give themselves completely to the redemptive task of emptying the systems of the world of their ungodly power through identifying with God in Christ.[8] It's a call to live with radical "power-in-vulnerability,"[9] as scholar Sarah Coakley notes, fully embracing one's marginalized identities as rooted in God's creativity, and using that identity as a powerful tool to expose the ungodly systems of the world and articulate a more just and equal vision of the kingdom of God.

This perspective still requires sacrifice—the sacrifice of fighting for one's own dignity and equity, as well as the dignity and equity of the world. It is a sacrifice to expose powers and systems that are fundamentally opposed to one's very existence, which is a great risk. The promise of Christ is that when we are willing to step up, to find our own divine strength in our God-crafted identities, and to work for the collective liberation of all beings, we will enter the most potent flow of truly transformative power, one that will ultimately result in our exaltation with and in Christ. As Coakley notes, kenosis "is not a negation of self, but the place of the self's transformation and expansion into God."[10]

The Kenosis Hymn uses the image of Christ's crucifixion as the pinnacle of Jesus' self-emptying. While we will explore this in depth later, a cursory exploration is important now when considering the idea of sacrifice or self-emptying among those who are already marginalized. The crucifixion of Jesus was a result of the collusion of the religious establishment with the government to silence a political dissident. Jesus was gaining a large following and his message that exposed the religiopolitical powers as corrupt caused fear of a revolution. Jesus knew that his message and example that empowered the dispossessed was dangerous, and he knew that it would likely result in his death. Yet he continued to preach. He continued to lean into his identity, his calling. He continued to empty himself of any hope of worldly power or privilege to advocate for a more just world.

When Jesus is finally arrested, he goes without resistance because he knows that in this moment he can expose the corruption of the systems of power most clearly. As he stands before Pilate, he allows the governor to struggle by giving clear, concise answers to his questions. He shows that he has done nothing wrong. In fact, he shows that he is truly *right*. Yet Pilate is more concerned with maintaining his political status—allowing a revolution to erupt in Israel would almost certainly cost him his job. So he hands over an innocent man to be killed, sacrificing him to appease his true god: power.

As Jesus is beaten and ultimately hung on the cross, he speaks no ill words toward anyone. He doesn't curse the empire or the religious establishment. In fact, he begs God to have mercy upon them. In the moment of his death, as the world looks on, the righteous son of God fully unmasks the primary evil of the world, then and now: our pursuit of becoming god. The ego of empire and of anyone who has privilege will do literally anything to maintain its position, even slaughtering innocent people who are simply seeking their own right to life and freedom. At the moment of his death, Jesus has fully and finally emptied himself in order to demonstrate the delusion of the pursuit of power and privilege. Its end is always death.

Whether one considers Jesus a historical prophet or the incarnation of God, it is nearly universally accepted that he intended to teach the world something profound through his willingness to be killed by the empire—and he clearly did. When we abstract the meaning of the cross into theologies of atonement, we strip it of its true meaning and potency. I think this is precisely why the apostle Paul *does* abstract the cross so often in his writing—he wanted his new religion to gain traction within the Roman Empire, so it was best not to focus on how that very empire killed Jesus unjustly.

Where Paul's theology does get Jesus' death right is in the belief that this kind of sacrifice was meant to be done "once for all" (Rom. 6:10). It's not meant to be repeated to make people right with God. It was intended to teach us that the pursuit and conservation of power and privilege always ends in death. It is a lesson that we are intended to learn through reflection upon it.

Therefore, any theology that requires individuals, especially the marginalized, to literally sacrifice themselves is missing the point. Christ did that gruesome work so that we wouldn't have to. The cross is intended to be our constant reminder of the faulty operating system of the world, and our inspiration to live in an alternative way. We're supposed to respond to the cross by fighting to defend those innocent reflections of Christ whom empire continues to crucify, to lynch, to lock up, and to abuse in our day. We're supposed to sacrifice our comfortable position within the status quo to dare to create the world that the prophets dreamed of.

Sometimes, following Christ's example *will* require us to put our lives on the line for the good of others. Sometimes we will be forced to face political, legal, and physical danger to stand up for ourselves and others. But most of the time, the call of the Kenosis Hymn will look like a call to lean into our God-crafted identities with bravery and vulnerability, refusing to be subject to corrupt systems that seek to marginalize us and others, and willing to put in the work to expose the lies and rebuild a reality built on the deepest truths of the gospel. Kenosis invites us to subject ourselves ultimately only to God and to systems that reflect God's heart for the world, enacting salvation through attitudes of service to the collective good of all of creation.

This is the paradoxology of it all: God's glory is revealed in our willingness to embrace ourselves, expose corruption, and serve one another—which is precisely the opposite message of the narrative perpetuated in each generation as power, privilege, and status are sought through conformity, corruption, and exploitation. Truly the apostle Paul was right in stating that the wisdom of the gospel is "foolishness to those who are perishing, but to us who are being saved it is the power of God" (1 Cor. 1:18).

DISCUSSION QUESTIONS

1. Have you thought about the political implications of Jesus' ministry? Has there been an emphasis on this teaching in any faith space you've been in?
2. How has sacrificial language been used in harmful ways in religious spaces you've been a part of?
3. Do you agree with the author that the actions and teachings of Jesus are well within our strength to do? Why or why not?
4. There is much debate in Christianity about faith versus works. How do you understand the balance between these two in your life?
5. Why is it so difficult for Christians to live into the teachings of Jesus both personally and politically?
6. How do we avoid asking those who are already vulnerable and oppressed to further humble themselves in the name of Jesus?

Chapter 3

A NEW MINDSET

Have the same way of thinking within you that
was also within Christ Jesus.
—Philippians 2:5, au. trans.

The journey of faith always moves from an inward to outward direction. Usually faith begins with an experience,
something that causes us to believe for a moment that there
is something more going on in the universe than we first
expected—perhaps a Creator who cares for us, or at the
very least an ordering principle behind everything that
exists. In other words, faith is born in the mind (or spirit,
heart, whatever you prefer to call it)—that mysterious place
within us where our consciousness resides. In Jesus' own
teaching, he consistently called his disciples to adopt a new
way of *seeing* the world before they could *enter* the new
reality that God was seeking to create. In other words, if
you want to experience the renewal of your own life and of
the world, it begins with how you think.

Paul precedes his quotation of the Kenosis Hymn
with the command to "have the same way of thinking [or
mindset] within you that was also within Christ Jesus."
From where Paul stands, everything that Jesus is described
as doing in the Kenosis Hymn began with a mindset. Jesus
had to adopt a way of thinking, commit to a way of perceiv-
ing, and, in some sense, commit to a belief that God's wisdom was truly the *best* way, even if it does seem to be foolish
from a natural perspective.

So much of our experience is shaped by our mindset. From very early in our lives, we are trained to begin thinking about ourselves and how we are to relate to the world, and those experiences in childhood form the foundation for how we think and act throughout the rest of our lives. Depending on where you were born, what your identity is, what sort of family system you entered, and a plethora of other factors, the worldview you begin to formulate will look very different. For me, as someone who grew up as a white, cisgender, gay boy in a working-class home in one of the wealthiest nations ever to exist, the way I learned to move in the world was contradictory.

On one hand, from very early on I heard that I could do anything I set my mind to and saw real-life examples of material success all around me in my teachers, in my friends' parents, and at church. My community also was infused with racist undertones; whenever a family of color moved into our trailer park, there was always a deep sense of suspicion toward them. When a large Mexican family moved into a mobile home across the street from ours, the whole neighborhood became abuzz with gossip about who they were and what they must be doing in that house. Our families immediately adopted racist stereotypes and assumed them to be true, and that impacted how we as kids interacted with the adults of that family and their children.

In this environment, I learned what it meant to be a man—a rugged, hard-working, dominant person, who probably liked to drink a lot and didn't respect his wife as an equal. Everything in my environment was hypersexualized—many of my friends had regular access to pornography at an early age, which shaped how they thought and behaved in relation to others. Despite the hard work (usually manual labor) that the men in my life engaged in, as soon as they got off the clock, they seemed to lack any real sense of responsibility. They lived to get home, crack open a twelve-pack of beer, and drink themselves into a stupor. I also picked up a belief that to show emotion or anything understood to be "feminine" was bad—even though I myself was shy, sensitive, and really enjoyed most of the things that were labeled "girlie."

Just these few environmental factors began to shape my young brain in ways that created a worldview that was both highly privileged and yet deeply repressed. I walked through the world knowing that I was a white man, and therefore, I could do anything, be anything, and didn't really have to fear anything. Intertwined with the racist undertones of the language I heard in my neighborhood was a subtle message of superiority—we were somehow better than others because we were white.

On the other hand, I couldn't hide my "femininity"— I was the skinniest boy around, had a soprano-toned voice, preferred to hang out with girls, and used to pretend I was Lizzie McGuire.[1] This led to intense bullying throughout my childhood and the overwhelming sense that there was something fundamentally wrong with me because I couldn't be like all the other boys.

I walked within this tension, and these identities began to form the mindset I engaged the world with.

Every single person has similar stories to share. Our early experiences shape our worldview, and we begin to live by the unspoken rules, standards, and biases that we were given. If we live an unexamined life, the mindset we inherited will remain with us throughout our lives, and we will live by the version of reality that it creates without ever allowing for the idea that there are other ways to view the world. And while it is true that every person's fundamental identity and worldview is as unique as their fingerprint, there are also group mindsets that are formed among people of similar identities, which reinforce the perceived truthfulness of an inherited perspective.

The 2016 US presidential election shocked many people. After the country was led for eight years by its first Black president and experienced leaps forward in social progress, few people could conceive that a far-right reality-show host could become the president and unleash a tidal wave of racism, sexism, transphobia, Islamophobia, and xenophobia in America. Yet this is precisely what happened. One of the reasons for Donald Trump's political success was his ability to tap into the ingrained group mindset of white voters, reinforcing the beliefs they had inherited in their upbringing but that had been suppressed as the culture progressed and began to look down on such beliefs and ideas. His simple messaging triggered the memory of a time when life was "easier" for white people, because we were not being challenged on our racism, sexism, or homophobia, and he promised to return the country to such an era.

As Trump used simple, racist, and xenophobic language on a global stage, many white people began to feel as though their mindsets were being legitimized once again. Instead of being challenged to examine the validity of their beliefs and perspectives, they were encouraged to simply embrace them as true, which resulted in a tidal wave of extreme racism and bigotry being unleashed by literal mobs at Trump campaign rallies, and then into communities across the country. Less than a year after his election, mobs of young, anti-Semitic white supremacists marched into Charlottesville, Virginia, holding tiki torches and shouting old Nazi slogans like "Blood and soil" and "Jews will not replace us." Many other white Americans watched in horror, wondering how this could be happening in our country in 2017, while most communities of color responded with a deep sense of anger and validation of what they had always known to be true—that the inherited mindset of white supremacy had never truly been rooted out of America, but had merely been suppressed and had finally reemerged.

While it's easy to look at these examples as extreme, the truth is that the potential for some variation of this behavior lies within all of us. All of us have inherited beliefs and perspectives that, if not carefully examined, will cause us to see the world in ways that are harmful to ourselves and to others. If you're a white person, a straight person, a cisgender male-identified person, an able-bodied person, or a Christian, it is almost certain that you were formed in such a way that these identities were deeply validated and valued, while other identities were spoken of as less than at best, worthy of oppression and exclusion at worst. This internal elitism gives birth to many of the major, systemic injustices in the world today but also results in day-to-day actions that hurt, offend, or disrespect others and the God who created them.

DISCIPLESHIP IS DOING

So how can we begin to shift our inherited beliefs and values to align more with the values of equity and inclusion? This is where discipleship becomes real. For far too many Christians, adopting the identity of "Christian" is primarily about believing a set of doctrines about who Jesus was, what he did in his life, and where we're going when we die. But this is a far cry from what Jesus himself understood to be the heart of discipleship. In his final commission to his disciples, Jesus proclaimed: "Go therefore and make disciples of all nations, baptizing them in the name of the Father and of the Son and of the Holy Spirit, and teaching them to obey everything that I have commanded you" (Matt. 28:19-20). Jesus' instruction to his disciples was twofold: to proclaim the good news, which he summarized as the proclamation that God was at work in the world bringing about redemption and restoration to all things, and then to actively teach people—not about theology, doctrines, or rituals, but to *obey* all that he commanded his disciples to *do*.

For Jesus, discipleship was about *doing*. It was about a new way of *living* in the world that brought about tangible justice and equity "on earth as it is in heaven." But before people can live out the way of Jesus, they must adopt the *mindset* of Jesus. They must actively work to begin thinking like Jesus, viewing others the way Jesus viewed them, and analyzing the world through the same eyes as the renegade rabbi from Nazareth. While the remainder of the Kenosis Hymn does a fairly good job of summarizing what exactly the "mind of Christ" looks like when it's embodied, it would serve us well to take some time to examine the life of Jesus and begin to get a full picture of how he thought and engaged in his world so that we might begin adopting this mindset as our own.

One of the most complete pictures of how Jesus viewed the world is articulated in his Sermon on the Mount, which is perhaps the most comprehensive summary of Jesus' primary teachings that we have. (Most scholars suggest that Jesus didn't teach all these things to his disciples in one sitting on a mountainside; rather, the author of the Gospel of Luke presented many of the primary teachings of Christ in one semilogical format for the sake of the reader.)

As disciples of Jesus, those who seek to embody his way of seeing and engaging in the world, we would do well to read through this sermon and ask not only *how we can live out these teachings in our context* but also, *What is the mindset behind each of the commands?* As those trying to understand how Jesus saw the world, we could do no better than to begin here.

At the beginning of this sermon, Jesus offers a series of subversive maxims that articulate his unique way of understanding the world and how God interacts with it. We call these the Beatitudes. These maxims come in the form of blessings, each of which has some basis in the Hebrew Bible, but to which Jesus adds a surprising twist. The word "beatitude" literally means "state of bliss" and is derived from the Latin *beatitudo,* which means "blessed." In this series of maxims, Jesus blesses unlikely groups of people, promising them tremendous rewards. These blessings would have been disconcerting to many of those who heard these statements in first-century Palestine, just as they are to many today. At their heart, they show us a picture of how Jesus understood the proper way of seeing and being in the world.

"Blessed are you who are poor, for yours is the kingdom of God." (Luke 6:20)

This first maxim gives us a glimpse into how Jesus viewed the economic system of his day. The economic system of first-century Palestine has interesting parallels to the modern American economic system, though its disparities were in some ways much harsher. Most of the population—about 90 percent—were a part of the peasant class,[2] which mainly consisted of those who worked the land to provide for their

own families and for the elite classes, which consisted primarily of Roman officials, aristocrats, and religious leaders.
A minority of the peasant class was engaged in the second-
ary means of income generation, trade, which capitalized
on goods and services exported throughout the broader
Roman Empire. The peasant class was forced to pay high
taxes, which were then used by the elites for their own purposes, leaving most of the Palestinian people unable to gain
any sort of economic mobility and destined for a life on the
edge of utter poverty.

Some did live in abject poverty. Those who suffered
from mental or physical illness, widows, and those who had
been socially marginalized for other reasons would have no
means of gaining an income or provision for themselves
other than through the rare welfare from state or religious
leaders, or from the almsgiving throughout Palestine. For
a person in the worst state of poverty, there was almost
no hope for escaping this economic and social fate in this
lifetime.

With knowledge of the cultural context that Jesus
was living and teaching in, we gain a bit more perspective
on the power of his teaching in this first beatitude. First,
he blesses those in poverty. Those who heard this teaching
might have heard it as a blessing of *their people* who were
living under the oppressive thumb of the Roman Empire,
while also likely knowing that there were those who were
far more economically deprived than themselves. Regardless of how the audience may have understood who exactly
was included in Jesus' blessing of "the poor," to look in
the eyes of an oppressed person and declare that "you are
blessed" seems, on the surface, like a harsh thing to do.
Nothing about their situation fits the traditional understanding of "blessing." But in the latter half of the maxim,

Jesus contextualizes this blessing: "for yours is the kingdom of God."

To the first-century Jewish listener, the idea of the "kingdom of God" was familiar. The idea of a messianic kingdom is referenced often in the Hebrew Bible and represented the day when God would overturn the oppressive empires of the world and establish a new world of justice, equity, and peace for all of humanity. The writers of the Mishnah, the commentary of early Jewish rabbis on the Torah, understood and hoped that the kingdom of God would appear when the oppressive Roman Empire fell. The Mishnah states, "When the Kingdom of Rome has ripened enough to be destroyed, the Kingdom of God will appear."[3] So when Jesus proclaimed that "the time is fulfilled, and the kingdom of God is at hand" (Mark 1:15 NKJV), his audience would have heard him declaring that Rome was about to fall and the long-awaited divine kingdom of David was about to be established. Presumably, they would have understood Jesus to be making a messianic claim, saying that he was going to be God's anointed king who would bring about peace, justice, and righteousness in the emerging new ordering of the world.

The attitude of Christ that is modeled in this text is one that is engaged deeply in the transformation of the systems of *this world*. It's a mindset that always focuses on the margins, seeking to find ways to make this beatitude a reality for those who are economically dispossessed. As Jesus spoke these words, the kingdom of God was not at all visible to most of the poor who would hear these words. But Jesus didn't only speak nice promises about some day in the distant future when economic justice would become a reality—he embodied a posture of economic justice in his day-to-day life and was not afraid to call out those in power who exploited the poor for their own financial gain. If we are going to adopt the attitude of Christ, we must be willing to do the same.

For the kingdom of God to become a reality, those of us who claim to follow Jesus must be willing to adopt *this* attitude—one that sees the poor as worthy of receiving the very comfort that we enjoy. It's an attitude that resists snap judgments about those in poverty and instead sees them as our equals, deserving of all the blessings and benefits that we enjoy. It's a mindset that recognizes our abundant wealth and is willing to freely give to those in need without a second thought, that is willing to pay higher taxes so that others can receive basic health care and living provisions, and that is increasingly mindful of how we utilize our resources.

"Blessed are you who hunger now, for you will be satisfied." (Luke 6:21a NIV)

In this beatitude, Jesus builds upon the theme of the first. Jesus blesses those who are hungry, or more literally, those who are *famished,* desperately yearning for basic food to eat. He promises that in the kingdom of God, they will be satisfied, or literally *fattened.* In essence, Jesus is declaring that in the world that God is creating through him, the reality of the oppressed will be reversed—from extreme hunger to extreme satisfaction.

It is important, once again, to remember the historical context of who Jesus was and where he was speaking this powerful statement. Jesus was first and foremost a religiopolitical revolutionary. He believed himself to be the one whom God had anointed to help liberate the Jewish people from the oppression of the corrupt Roman Empire. In this context, even the poorest Roman citizens were offered basic food rations either free or for a low price, while those who lived in occupied territories were essentially responsible for themselves. So when Jesus speaks these words, he is speaking to a crowd that is desperately hungry. He is speaking to parents who worry *every day* about what their children are going to eat. He is speaking words that would be received by his listeners as not merely a heartwarming promise of future redemption, but revolutionary words that would have caused the crowd to stand on their feet and cry out in agreement.

Jesus came not merely to deliver a message to people who were in low spirits, but to outline a sociopolitical path that would result in equity and justice for a people who lived under cruel oppression. These words in the Beatitudes come at the beginning of Jesus' public ministry and serve as a lens through which we should view everything else that he did. Jesus' attitude was one that was seeking to create an environment in which those who were starving would be given enough food to make them full. The undergirding mindset here is that Jesus also knew that there was *more than enough* food to make this a reality. Not only did Jesus know this, but the starving people did too. They likely heard stories of lavish imperial feasts in Rome and witnessed Roman citizens in their land having wonderful full meals whenever they'd like. As happens today, they probably witnessed a great deal of food waste, and their hearts broke as they saw means to feed their families be wasted by careless people. This was Jesus' own reality as well; as a peasant Jewish man, he likely spoke these words with the grumbling of hunger in his own stomach.

The attitude of Jesus revealed in this beatitude is that there is more than enough to go around. There is more than enough to ensure that everyone is filled. And it is not enough just to believe this—those who follow Christ must be willing to work hard to make this a reality in our own communities, countries, and around the world. The kingdom of God is not an unattainable reality—it's fairly easy to make the Beatitudes come true. The problem is that humans are deeply plagued by greed, which causes us to stockpile resources for our own good that may eventually expire while others suffer with no resources available to them. Most of us live with far more than we need, and others live with nothing at all. The poverty rates in the United States reveal just how deeply we are infected with greed: in a nation that has the largest economy in the world, in 2018 an estimated 11.1 percent of US households lived with food insecurity, meaning that about 14.3 million households (roughly as many households as in Texas and Ohio combined) did not have enough food each day.[4]

While the modern world is much better at hiding just how much hunger exists around us, the truth is that far too many people are needlessly suffering in our world while many of us live with more than enough. If we are to adopt the mindset of Christ, we must begin by taking a deep look at our own use of resources—food, money, government resources, and so on—and asking how can we leverage our access to abundance to ensure that those struggling to eat one meal each day can be well fed.

**"Blessed are you who weep now, for you will laugh."
(Luke 6:21b)**

Once again, for this beatitude, historical context is everything. Jesus is preaching to a severely oppressed people. A people who were deeply accustomed to weeping. A people who were deeply accustomed to revolutionaries like Jesus who came along proclaiming a better future and organizing an uprising against Rome only to be brutally executed in the sight of their hopeful followers. The people of first-century Palestine, just like the people of Palestine today, were often taunted by hope but rarely saw it come to fruition. Jesus is speaking to a people who lived in a land that had been saturated by tears for centuries, and so for him to look these folks in the eyes and say, "Blessed are you who weep" would have been most disconcerting.

The attitude of Jesus on display here is one of persistent hope in the face of hopeless situations. Again, neither Jesus nor the people he was preaching to had any *real* reason to hope. Theirs was a story of always *almost* getting to the "promised land," only to be told that they would never actually reach it. Throughout the Hebrew Bible, the Jewish people consistently are brought into moments of victory only to have it taken away by God, by their enemies, or by their own actions. And yet, one thing that can surely be said about the Jewish people is that in the face of constant disappointment, their hope is persistent. They believe that God made a promise to their forefather Abraham and that God will fulfill that promise, come hell or high water.

In this beatitude we find Jesus mirroring this attitude of hope back to his people, acknowledging their grief and pain and inviting them to continue yearning for a day when their sorrows would be turned not just to joy, but to exuberant laughter. One of the most consistent qualities of Jesus throughout the Gospel accounts is his remarkable ability to empathize with those who are suffering while also keeping an eye toward a better tomorrow. Jesus consistently gets down in the dust and the dirt of the real pain and suffering of people and doesn't merely spout off religious platitudes, but sheds tears with them and for them.

But in every single one of these examples, Jesus doesn't allow sorrow to have the last word. While he is not afraid to shed tears in solidarity with those who are suffering, he always gives them a reason to maintain hope. The miracles of Jesus were meant to be a taste of what life in God's kingdom would be like—every miracle is an example of Jesus taking something broken by human sinfulness and subverting it for the good of those on the margins. When Jesus multiplies the bread and fish to feed the masses, the message is that in God's economy, everyone is provided for. When Jesus heals those who are ill or raises the dead, the message is that everyone will be cared for and will live long, abundant lives in the new world God is creating. When Jesus finds the wine jars empty and fills them with the highest-quality wine, the message is that in God's kingdom the celebration will never be over. In every instance he is reminding us that the world was not meant to be this way and that it doesn't have to stay this way. Change can happen, and indeed already is happening, slowly but surely.

The mindset of Jesus does not fear the pain and grief of the marginalized and broken, but rather kneels down and sits in it. At the same time, it doesn't merely offer empathy, but also seeks to find tangible ways to turn tears of sorrow into tears of laughter, to not just console but to cure the ills that ail them. It's an attitude of persistent hopefulness that is not only willing to dream of a better tomorrow but that also works to make that better tomorrow a reality today. Jesus embodied this radical compassion in nearly every encounter he had—he didn't offer merely platitudes and a pat on the shoulder, but active empathy that sought to change the circumstances of the marginalized person in the here and now.

If we are to embody the mindset embedded in this beatitude, we must be willing to inconvenience ourselves, get uncomfortable, and make sacrifices in our own lives to bring about the betterment of others. Throughout the Bible, there is a constant refrain: faith without works is meaningless. The mindset of Christ in this beatitude provokes us not to merely be a people of vain religious platitudes, but in every circumstance when we are confronted with those who are weeping to consider if there is a way to both empathize and transform the persons' circumstances to bring about justice and joy. There may not always be something that we can do, but we have the responsibility to look within ourselves to consider how we can dry the tears of the oppressed, transforming them to laughter once and for all.

FILLED TO BE EMPTIED

These three authentic beatitudes of Jesus give us a true glimpse into how Jesus saw the world. He was on a mission to set things right, not just in a spiritual sense, but in the real world that he lived in. Early in the Christian movement, these beatitudes began to be "spiritualized" because even some early Christians realized just how radical the mindset that Jesus embodied was, and how difficult for us to adopt. (Look at the same beatitudes in Matthew's Gospel and you'll see the introduction of phrases like "poor in spirit," which fundamentally changes the original, real-world meaning of the Beatitudes of Jesus.)

When one views the message of the historical Jesus, divorced from the later theologizing of the apostle Paul and subsequent generations of theologians, it's hard to see Jesus embodying anything less than a movement of social transformation for the oppressed people of first-century Palestine. His was a gospel of resistance to the oppressive forces of the Roman Empire. His was a message of subversive transformation of the world from the bottom up. And his example required anyone who desired to follow him to adopt a lifestyle of action and sacrifice—working daily to transform the kingdoms of this world into the kingdom of God on earth as in heaven.

Many people may rightly ask how this reading of Jesus' mindset and mission squares with the spiritual aspects of Jesus' teachings and the later teachings of his apostles. In fact, the apostle Paul spills much ink trying to reiterate to the early churches that following Jesus has very little to do with *works* and everything to do with receiving God's *grace*. While this has traditionally been understood by Christians as an invitation to adopt Christianity as primarily a private religious practice, I believe this interpretation is not only inaccurate, but has allowed Christianity to become a tool of the imperial systems that Jesus spent his life railing against.

In nearly every teaching that comes from Jesus' lips, there is an imperative to action. The faith of Jesus is anything but a private piety, and this is one of the reasons why some of the religious leaders in his day opposed him so intensely. Jesus was advocating for a faith that was manifested not primarily in religious ceremony or ritual, but in principled actions that brought actual change—which made Jesus the target of imperial forces, and this jeopardized the standing of other Jewish religious leaders if they couldn't quiet Jesus down. Jesus was seeking to incite a revolution— but it was in a very different path from all the other Jewish revolutionaries in his day. He was encouraging a progressive, grassroots transformation of society through forming communities that overturned injustice one subversive act of love and charity at a time.

This doesn't negate, however, that Jesus' gospel had an internal, spiritual dimension as well. To be primed for a life of action, Jesus spent much time cultivating a vibrant inner life through practices that connected him to God. In Luke, Jesus warns about those who would declare that the kingdom of God—the world as God intended it to be—was "appearing" in certain places and times:

> Once, on being asked by the Pharisees when the kingdom of God would come, Jesus replied, "The coming of the kingdom of God is not something that can be observed, nor will people say, 'Here it is,' or 'There it is,' because the kingdom of God is within you." (17:20–21 NIV)

This teaching has been misconstrued in many ways throughout the ages, often to teach that the kingdom of God is *merely* a spiritual inner state and not an external reality. What Jesus is saying here, in the context of all his other teachings, seems to be that the reality of the kingdom *begins* internally and then is manifested externally, over time. Whenever Jesus speaks of the kingdom, he uses analogies of slow progress. For instance, in Mark 4:30–32 he says the kingdom is like a seed that is planted and over many generations grows into a beautiful tree. The idea is that when we are rightly connected to God, receiving God's nourishment and instruction, we will become those who are planting and watering the seeds of the kingdom. Through a constant centering of our spirits on God's peace and light, we are filled and empowered to be able to cultivate the seeds of the kingdom in the real world.

This aspect of establishing the kingdom in the world is just as crucial as the action we are called to embody in our inner lives. Throughout history, however, the way of Jesus has become spiritualized to the detriment of actual social transformation, which is why I feel compelled to make the strong case for a socially active faith. But it's also true that if we are not constantly ensuring that we are tethered to the reality of the kingdom of God within ourselves, then we will grow tired, cynical, and ultimately hopeless in our pursuit of a more just world. Again, when we're talking about the kingdom, we're talking about God's intended ordering of things.

CULTIVATING THE KINGDOM WITHIN

Externally, God's kingdom is the world as it was intended to function, a world of provision and peace for all of creation that is so beautifully illustrated in the myth of Eden in Genesis. Internally, it is God's intended ordering of our souls, where we have aligned our inner world with the flow of peace and deep connection to God that is illustrated in the relationship of Adam and Eve with God before the fall of humanity. In the Genesis story, we are told that Adam and Eve live in union with God without shame or hiding (Gen. 2:25). Their souls are laid bare before God, and there is a deep sense of intimacy with their Creator. They know their purpose—to take care of the garden (Gen. 2:15)—and they live in true *shalom*, a Hebrew word that literally means "wholeness." This inner state experienced by Adam and Eve in the creation myth is the inner state we too are invited to experience. But for us, this state of shameless peace, purpose, and connection to God is not at all natural—it takes a lot of practice.

God desires justice not only within our world, but also within our souls. The mindset of Christ Jesus that Paul talks about at the very beginning of the Kenosis Hymn is one of inner shalom. Jesus was able to be an effective agent of the kingdom of God externally precisely because he took the necessary time to ensure that he was being filled with the shalom of God internally. How often do we read in the Gospel accounts that Jesus withdraws from the crowds, pauses his miracle working, and takes time to pray, to meditate in nature, and to rest? Luke 5:16 (NLT) tells us that "Jesus often withdrew to the wilderness for prayer." These words come immediately after we're told that "crowds of people came to hear him and to be healed of their sicknesses" (v. 15 NIV). In the moments that were arguably the height of his popularity, the pinnacle of his organizing and justice work, instead of pushing himself to the point of burnout, Jesus turned from the crowds, went into nature, and prayed.

Such discipline takes a lot of faith. Oftentimes, as we seek to live into whatever God has called us to, when we begin to see success or increased impact, it is very hard to practice self-care. In moments of crisis we may feel that it is irresponsible for us to prioritize our own inner life. Jesus shows us that regardless of what is happening, we must prioritize our own inner shalom. Sick people needed his healing—he still took time to disconnect. Demon-possessed people were suffering—he still took time to rest. Folks whose hope had been utterly crushed desperately needed a word of encouragement—he still retreated into the wilderness. You see, the principle of self-sacrifice and pouring out is often misconstrued in unhealthy ways. It may seem counterintuitive, but self-sacrifice doesn't require you to sacrifice *yourself*. It means you're willing to make sacrifices in your life for the good of others, but the only way to remain effective in doing so in the long term is to prioritize your inner well-being.

The mindset of Christ lives in this tension: always scanning one's surroundings for ways that justice, healing, and peace could be spread, while also scanning one's inner self to ensure that there is peace and connection to the Source. At the end of the day, Christians believe that it is God who is ultimately at work in us and through us (Phil. 2:13). We believe that we are but channels through which God spreads redemption and reconciliation in the world. If we are not continually tapping back into God and reenergizing through rest, we will *always* become ineffective at our work. In justice work, there are so many people who become impassioned about a cause, throw themselves into it, but very quickly become weary, cynical, and, frankly, harmful to the very cause they are seeking to help.

Humans are not made to run 24/7; we are not made to always be producing or giving or creating. Jesus understood this, much to his overly zealous disciples' chagrin. Do you remember the story in Mark 4 in which Jesus is sleeping in a boat as a storm arises and his disciples are running around terrified? The groggy Jesus wakes up, slightly annoyed at the disciples, and simply calms the storm. This is a metaphor for so much of our lives. There will always be something to do, somewhere to serve, someone who we think *needs* our attention. Nevertheless, we *must* prioritize our own inner peace and well-being. The storm will be calmed, the needs will get met, and our taking a nap is not going to prevent that from happening. Taking time to pray or meditate is not going to cause the ship to sink. While we must never allow ourselves to become selfish or complacent, if we can't cultivate wholeness within ourselves, we will never be effective at cultivating it anywhere else. If we are going to truly live as disciples of Christ, then adopting Jesus' mindset is the first and most essential step. To know Jesus' mindset requires getting to know Jesus, through his example and teachings in the Gospels. There we will witness the masterful way in which Jesus continually examined his world, seeking to overturn injustice at every chance, while also taking time to ensure that he remained connected to God and filled with the energy, faith, and clarity he needed to be effective in the world.

In the rest of this book, we're going to walk through the Kenosis Hymn as a summary of how Jesus lived his life and how we, as disciples, should as well. But this is just the starting point. As disciples of Jesus, we should make a regular practice of studying those red letters in our Bibles as often as possible, because they are filled with layers of wisdom and insight for how exactly we can establish the shalom of God within ourselves and in the world around us. We must continually return to fill our minds with Christ's wisdom so that we can then pour it out as his hands and feet in the world. This is, after all, what it *truly* means to be a Christian.

DISCUSSION QUESTIONS

1. How would you describe your mindset when it comes to viewing people of another gender, race, or socioeconomic status? What beliefs shape the way you see them?
2. How would you describe the way Jesus saw the world and the various peoples in it?

3. What do you think it means for the poor, hungry, and grieving to be blessed?
4. Which beatitude do you find to be most challenging to accept? Which is most challenging for our society?
5. What does the term "kingdom of God" mean to you? How is life in the kingdom of God different from our present world?
6. What are some practices that help you to cultivate inner wholeness, or "the kingdom within"? What connection do these practices have to the way you live out your faith externally?

Chapter 4

OWNING OUR IDENTITY

. . . who existed in the form of God and was
equal with God, yet did not consider that his
equality with God was something that should
be seized for his own benefit.
—Philippians 2:6, au. trans.

Privilege is usually invisible to those who have it until it's
called out. Most people do not like to acknowledge that
they possess privilege because they feel as if it invalidates
their life experience or efforts to become who they are. In
our world today, it seems that privilege has become a dirty
word. But what if privilege, in and of itself, weren't necessarily a bad thing? The truth is that in every country, culture, and community that has ever existed, certain groups
of people were given privileges based on their identities and
others were not. Privileges extended to citizens of a country, for instance, are withheld from those who are merely
visitors. The system is set up to benefit one group of people
and not another. We'd never call that immoral—it's simply
how social ordering works. Social hierarchies are a necessary part of the ordering of society, and as long as there
is hierarchy, there will be those with more privilege and
power than others.

When we talk about privilege in the Western world
today, things get a bit murkier, however. Many Western
nations have been notorious colonizers, explicitly moti-
vated by white supremacy, patriarchy, and distorted ideas

of Christianity, resulting in systems that not only exclude certain groups of people, but actively oppress and degrade their humanity. The way we have constructed our social privilege in America, for instance, requires us to take a hard look at the unjust ideologies that undergird it and actively seek to dismantle them for the sake of people of color in our nation. The founding treatises of America have racism interwoven through them openly—the Declaration of Independence refers to the indigenous people of America as "merciless Indian Savages." While the same document declares that "all men are created equal, that they are endowed by their Creator with certain unalienable Rights, that among these are Life, Liberty and the pursuit of Happiness," many of the founders did not have in mind Black people, the indigenous people of America, women, and many others who were not only either explicitly or implicitly excluded from their laws and early documents, but were actively abused and oppressed by them.

As a white American, it is crucial for me to educate myself on how our society came to be—beyond the mythologized version that we're often taught in school—and to wrestle with how I have benefited from the oppression of other people. We've already established that my own journey in life hasn't been easy—yours may not have been either—but I certainly have had more of a chance to rise above the poverty I was born into than most Black and Brown people with equal skill. My ability to establish a career as a writer is, at some level, tied to a social bias that works in my favor—white men are more likely to get book deals than women or people of color. But this isn't a reason, necessarily, for me not to pursue my dream and calling to write. Acknowledging your privilege doesn't mean, necessarily, that you need to surrender it completely and simply settle for less than the life you desire or work for. But it does mean that you need to examine your mindset, examine the ways you've benefited because of your privilege, and begin to think about how you can utilize your position to raise up marginalized people.

This directive is clearly portrayed in the Kenosis Hymn as Christ's own relationship to identity and power is described: he "existed in the form of God and was equal with God." This is a statement of description but it also suggests an internal sense of ownership of the identity: Jesus was *in the form of God* and was *equal with God*—this is a recognition of his identity and the privilege it conferred upon him. If we take this as a directive for our own lives, then it calls for us to take an honest look at our *form*, in Greek, *morphē*, or visible appearance. While not all our privileged statuses are related to outward form, many of them are. The early Christians confessed that Jesus was the "visible image of the invisible God" (Col. 1:15 NLT) and this physical form is what made him *equal with God*. Jesus' power and authority came from his *form*.

IDENTITY CHECK

Using Jesus as a metaphor for our own experience, we too would do well to examine how we show up in the world. In our culture today there is a common phrase used to describe this process: "checking your privilege." This awareness is the essential first step toward being able to utilize it in the service of the world. This phrase is sometimes used inappropriately to invoke guilt or shame in privileged groups of people; however, the directive behind it is one that we should take to heart. Most of us live unexamined lives in an unexamined world. We don't often think about the meta questions of who we *actually* are and how we got to where we're at today. But the invitation of Jesus is to enter into deep contemplation and reflection on these questions that then moves us to live in better ways.

How do we determine what areas of our identity confer privilege upon us in our society?

In 2014, the University of San Francisco launched a campus-wide campaign called "Check Your Privilege" that invited students to reflect upon the ways that they might experience privilege in their culture.[1] They identified six key areas of privilege within personal identities. Roughly speaking, those areas related to gender, sexuality, class, religion, disability, and race. To conduct a very surface-level assessment of one's privileges, one only needs to fill in their identity in each of those categories and ask, "Do people with this identity hold more power, positions, wealth, and status than other people do?" Let me demonstrate this by listing my own identities:

Gender: Cisgender male
Sexuality: Gay
Class: Middle
Religion: Christian
Disability: Able-bodied
Race: White

Based on these identities, it is safe to say that *most* of the people with power in my culture and country are fundamentally *like me*. This is not inherently wrong. This does not have to be inherently negative. The question is, however, are those without these identities blocked from equal access to resources in our society? In America, the answer is yes. I, like many white people in America, have ancestors who unjustly enslaved African people and used them to establish the country that I now live in. The legacy of slavery still exists today in the collective racism that exists in the consciousness of white Americans, and the government continues to perpetuate racist policies that keep Black and Brown folks from equality. As a person within the middle class, the hard truth is that in the current makeup of the society, my comfortable existence is supported by primarily people of color who have no choice but to work low-paying jobs that prevent them from climbing the class ladder. As a Christian, I can expect the country to honor my religious holidays with business closures and public decorations—and not the holidays of Muslims, Hindus, or Jews. As an able-bodied person, I don't have to think about whether spaces I enter are accessible to those who might experience disability. And as a cisgender man, I unconsciously operate with a sense of safety and dominance in the spaces that I enter. As a gay man, I do get a taste of what marginalization feels like. In many places in my country and around the world, I cannot simply exist with a partner without fear of violence or discrimination. At the time of writing, I can still be refused a job or housing because of my sexuality in more than half of the states in America.

These things are simply true. Their truthfulness isn't negated by the fact that I have struggled to get where I am today. They are not less true because my family endured great hardships to enable me to be where I am today. Again, the privilege itself is morally neutral. Contemplating our identity is important if we are to be aware of how we show up in the world. But such contemplation will often lead us to realize the sad truth that *many* of our privileged identities benefit us *not because of some inherent superiority* but because we have *actively oppressed others* to climb to the top of the social hierarchy. Sure, I work very hard to be antiracist in my daily life—but the truth is that my ancestors who migrated from England and settled in Virginia owned African slaves, whom they exploited and abused so that they could further my family's well-being. The only reason my white skin is of any benefit to me is precisely because my family and thousands of others intentionally, willfully, enslaved other human beings.

COLLECTIVE RESPONSIBILITY AND ACTION

What do we do with this knowledge? Many white people may respond, "Well, I cannot be held responsible for the sins of my fathers," but the truth is that if we don't take responsibility for them, likely, *we will perpetuate the sin.* Focusing only on the "present moment" is a modern phenomenon, and despite its usefulness as a meditation technique, it can become a selfish idea. For most of human history, individuals have seen themselves as the product of a long lineage of ancestors and as the progenitors of future generations. Our ancestors are within us—their wisdom and their sin—and we have a responsibility to future generations to pass on the wisdom and break the curse of generational sin. It may not seem fair to us in the moment, but that is only because we have bought into the toxic idea of hyperindividualism that says that the only thing that matters is our personal freedom and our personal progress.

The message of Jesus cuts right through this noise. While we are individuals with personal responsibilities, we must remember that we are also fundamental parts of a collective, and our individual actions have a direct impact on the well-being of the collective. This is why Jesus emphasized the unity of his followers so often—because unless we care for and consider each other, greed, exploitation, and selfishness will be the result. This is clearly no way to build the flourishing society or world that God intended. When we examine our privilege, we necessarily must examine our past and decide about the trajectory of the future, not only for ourselves but for generations to come. Do we want to perpetuate the oppression of others simply so we can have a comfortable existence, leaving the responsibility of repentance to future generations? Or do we want to heed Jesus' radical call to discipleship and begin the work of setting the world to right within our own lifetime?

I believe this is one of the reasons Jesus so often emphasized that the kingdom of God was to come *on earth as it was in heaven.* He called people to take their gaze off the afterlife and instead to focus on working to make their lives within this world reflective of the heaven that we all long for. The truth is that a more just and generous world is absolutely *within our reach,* if only we get serious about owning our privilege, repent of the sins we inherit and perpetuate, and actively utilize our position to dismantle systems of oppression and to uplift those who have been held down under the weight of our collective "flourishing." This is demonstrated when Paul writes that Jesus "did not consider that his equality with God was something that should be seized for his own benefit." Once there was an acknowledgment of a privileged identity, Jesus willingly used it *not primarily for his own benefit* but for the collective well-being of others.

As you examine your own identities, based on the simple list we used earlier, think of how not just *you* personally, but the collective of people who share a common identity with you have benefited due to the exploitation of that identity. If you are able-bodied, for instance, think about how almost every aspect of daily life has been literally *constructed* for our benefit but not for the benefit of those who are disabled. From the grocery stores we shop at, to the environments we work in, to the social expectations we have normalized—our society has largely been constructed without any consideration of the 19 percent of Americans who are disabled.[2] The kenotic path of Jesus calls us to take our focus off ourselves and to consider others before ourselves. We should continually be considering how we can make our disabled neighbors more welcome, more included, with an equal shot at flourishing in our communities as those of us who are able-bodied.

Through a collectivistic lens, we are always seeking to care for the *entire* community, not ignoring the needs of the minorities within our midst but giving special attention and care to them. One of Jesus' most beautiful parables is that of the wandering sheep in Matthew 18—Jesus leaves the ninety-nine other sheep to save the one who was wandering off. While not a perfect analogy, this parable demonstrates God's care not just for the majority but for each individual person. In a collective, personal identity and significance doesn't dissolve into one corporate identity, but rather enters an interconnected web of unique individuals who are all always seeking to care for, include, and value others. While the use of differences to divide fades when we acknowledge we are all ultimately a part of one human family, our unique identities should by no means be down-played—because when that happens, the majority identity always seems to dominate.

LIVING AN OTHER-CENTERED LIFE

One of the most counterintuitive truths of the Christian faith is that the path toward personal fulfillment begins and ends with taking our gaze off ourselves and focusing it on others. Nearly everything about our evolutionarily condi-tioned nature tells us otherwise—if we are to survive, we need to focus on ourselves first. We should focus on *our tribe, our family, our loved ones,* and not worry about every-one else. This has been a part of human consciousness since the very beginning of our existence and is one of the reasons we have flourished for so long as a species. But the call of Jesus is to rise above our conditioning and to reach for a higher level of consciousness. We're being called to make an evolutionary leap, beyond survival of the fittest to a new perspective on who we are and how we will flourish. As I stated above, this is a leap from an *individualistic* way of seeing the world to a *collectivistic* or even *cosmic* way of seeing the world.

One of my mentors is the world-renowned philoso-pher Ken Wilber, who developed Integral Theory, a way of understanding the evolution of human consciousness that has been deeply helpful across traditions and fields of study. One of the most popular tools that Ken has created is a simple map that shows how humanity as a whole and how we as individuals evolve in our worldview. Below is my rough reconstruction of Wilber's chart:[3]

Level of Consciousness	Primary Concern and Focus
6. Integral (Later Adulthood)	Seeking to include all perspectives as essential as an individual, collective, and cosmically
5. Pluralistic (Adulthood)	Seeking the collective good, multiple perspectives, and equality for all
4. Rational (Early Adulthood)	Seeking independence and a rational understanding of the world
3. Mythic (Adolescence)	Seeking to find authority, structure, and discipline in the world
2. Magic (Early Childhood)	Seeking to protect and defend the tribe or family
1. Archaic (Infancy)	Seeking the survival of the physical self

Beginning from the bottom of this chart and going to the top is an understanding of both how we as individuals progress throughout life in our perception of the world and how culture has evolved throughout the course of human history. According to Wilber, most of human culture is still at "rational" or lower levels of consciousness, and nearly all major religions function primarily below the rational level. The level of consciousness that Jesus was and is calling his disciples to, however, is akin to the "integral" level, or the ability to empathize and see value in every level of consciousness in ourselves, others, and society as a whole, and seeking to utilize the merits of each level for personal and collective well-being. This theory is not meant to be used as a *judgment* on other people, seeking to classify them as a "lower level" than us, but rather simply to observe the stages of consciousness that *all humans* tend to move through—and these stages have been well documented and affirmed by many leading psychologists, including Robert Keegan and James Fowler.[4]

I bring Wilber's theory into this conversation to demonstrate that many, if not most, people are functioning at a level of consciousness that draws us away from other-centered thinking. Even cultures that are in the "pluralistic" level of consciousness tend to be rather tribalistic, valuing only those who are their own level of consciousness and demonizing all those beneath them. Yet the path demonstrated by Jesus in the Kenosis Hymn requires us to work toward adopting an *integral perspective* on the world. We are to look toward others, regardless of how they view the world and what beliefs or ideologies they espouse, as people who are trying their best to live well with whatever stage of consciousness they adopt. We need to seek to empathize with those who view the world differently, and instead of disregarding them or demonizing them, we are to seek to use whatever privilege or power we have to *bless* them.

But again, it is likely that most of us do not view the world in an integral way, so this is going to take a lot of work, especially for those of us who benefit from great privilege or power in society—to be able to utilize what we have for the good of others, we're going to need to intentionally seek to rise above our conditioning and evolutionary impulses toward self-preservation and tribalism in order to be a blessing to others. For followers of Jesus, this isn't an optional practice—it is the *whole* of what it means to be a disciple. Jesus, who was equal to God, didn't exploit his status, his perspective, his power for his own benefit, but rather, he utilized it for the good of others. And in turn, he accessed the very thing that every human being is ultimately seeking: fulfillment.

In John 10:10, Jesus speaks these beautiful words: "I came so that everyone would have life, and have it in its fullest" (CEV). Note that Jesus doesn't say that he came so that we might go to heaven when we die, or that we might have our sins forgiven, but rather that his mission was to give everyone *life in its fullest.* This almost sounds like a line out of a modern self-help book, but the difference is that the teachings of Jesus don't lead us to focus on ourselves but on others. Jesus' entire life and ministry was defined by his willingness to serve others, and this clearly resulted in a level of inner peace and satisfaction that was contagious, which is why hundreds of people flocked to hear him preach whenever they had a chance.

If we are going to follow in the path of Jesus toward a fulfilled life, we must start by owning our privilege and then willfully choosing, at every chance we have, to utilize it for the benefit of those with less privilege. Not only will this result in justice and equity being established for others, but we too will finally tap into the deep fulfillment we all long for. This is not an easy path to walk, and our own conditioning and level of consciousness will pull us in exactly the opposite direction. This is why Jesus said that his followers must be willing to "deny themselves and take up their cross *daily* and follow me" (Luke 9:23, emphasis mine). The path of discipleship is a *daily* decision, a *daily* recommitment to believe that Jesus knew what he was talking about, a *daily* belief that we can work to create a more just and beautiful reality. It's a call to *deny ourselves and take up our cross*—which isn't a call to asceticism, but rather a call to owning who we are and the privileges we have and being willing to utilize them for others.

CHECKING IN

At this point in the book, it's important that we take a moment to check in. For many readers, what I've written thus far may not be very challenging—it may have you nodding in agreement. But the point of this book and the point of Jesus' ministry was not to give us powerful talking points that get us fired up, but to provoke us to *follow* them. It's easy to write these words and it's easy to read them. But the call to own our privilege and then to consciously utilize it for the good of others is *much harder to live out*. It requires us to choose to live with our eyes wide open to injustice and inequity around us and to be bold and brave enough to do something to fix it.

The following chapters will explore how Jesus did that, tangibly, in his day-to-day life, and how we can embrace his example in ours. As we proceed, I invite you not only to reflect deeply on these topics but also to begin to think about how to embody these principles in your life right now. Discipleship is a path of trial and error, a path of doing rather than simply espousing, so by the grace of God, I invite you into a posture of practice.

DISCUSSION QUESTIONS

1. What makes social hierarchies good (or morally neutral) and bad? How do you feel about claims of equality—such as in the US Declaration of Independence or our idealistic view of society—when reality shows so much inequality?
2. How does naming your identities make you feel? Do you believe that these aspects of your and others' identities are important? Why or why not?

3. When considering what to do with the knowledge of your own privilege and others' oppression, why is acknowledging these realities an important first step?

4. How can you follow Jesus' example of considering your privilege not "something that should be seized for [your] own benefit" but something to use for the benefit of others? How can we own our identity while following Jesus' call to deny ourselves?

5. How does an individual's stage of spiritual development impact the way they understand and use their identity?

6. Following the author's suggestion to "check in," how do you feel at this point in our journey, having faced some challenging truths and preparing to follow Jesus' challenging call to action?

Chapter 5

EXCHANGING ROLES

But he emptied himself, taking on the role of
the slave, born in human form.
                                  —Philippians 2:7a

We live in a culture that thrives on ego. Richard Rohr, an
expert in the Enneagram (a personality assessment with
ancient roots), says that the United States is a culture of
"Threes"—the personality type that thrives on projecting
an image of success, attractiveness, and prosperity, even
though that projection may not always align with their lived
reality. [1] Unhealthy Enneagram Threes want you to believe
that they're amazing high achievers, even if their success is
limited or came from taking shortcuts or distracting with
smoke and mirrors. Our culture conditions us to desire
success more than anything else, and success is usually
defined by wealth, fame, and social status.

   This ambition isn't unique to our culture—it's been
a prevalent temptation in cultures throughout human history. It's one of the reasons why Jesus was so despised by
so many people in the first century—he put a spotlight on
the shallow "prosperity" of the religious and political elite
and called all people to surrender the pursuit of these vain
rewards in exchange for a life of sacrificial service. In chapter 4 we examined how important it is for us to understand
our identities and how they work in our favor and against
other people. Now, as we continue to progress through the
Kenosis Hymn, we're challenged to *utilize* the benefits of
our identity, utilizing them for others.

In Philippians 2:7, we encounter the defining phrase of the hymn: "But he emptied himself." The word "to empty" here is the Greek *kenōsis* that we talked about at the very beginning of this book. It's a powerful word that both describes the fundamental posture of Jesus' own life and serves as the fundamental directive for anyone seeking to follow in his path.

EMPTYING OURSELVES

What does it mean to empty ourselves? If we study the example of Jesus, we can see two different examples of how this plays out. First, let's examine Jesus *theologically* as a person of absolute privilege. If we accept the theology of the hymn to be truthful and affirm that Jesus Christ is the incarnation of the Creator, "in the form of God" (v. 6), then it is fair to assert that he possessed absolute privilege and power. There is nothing he cannot do, there is nothing he cannot have, there is nothing he cannot create or become. Theologians would affirm that God is worthy of absolute sovereignty and it is our role to merely accept God's will. Kenosis challenges this idea in a fundamental way.

This passage of the hymn tells us that the one who *shares God's very nature* willingly chose to surrender his divine position, power, and privilege for the good of creation. The God revealed in Jesus is not one that revels in power and authority, but instead pours it out to bring redemption and restoration to the world. Jesus willingly limited himself, choosing not to utilize his power to escape suffering, loss, and pain, but rather entered into it fully in order to sympathize with the suffering of the world. Not only that, but Jesus chose to tap into his power and privilege *only* for the benefit of others—it is never used in a self-serving way in any of the Gospel accounts. We hear nothing about Jesus healing himself, feeding himself, or calling upon the angels of heaven to rescue him from an unjust trial and death. But we do hear of Jesus using his power to heal the most despised of his day—the Samaritan woman, the demoniac, tax collectors, and sinners.

What is so powerful about this particular verse is that it doesn't merely say that Jesus *poured himself out for others,* but it tells us that he absolutely *emptied* himself. He used every ounce of his power and privilege to benefit others. By the end of his life, he was an empty vessel. As followers of Jesus, we are called to take this same path. Our lives will be measured not by material success but by the way we gave of ourselves to make the world a little more just and a little more beautiful. Again, we know this to be true at a fundamental level. We don't hear people on their deathbeds boast about their positions or possessions—instead, people reflect on their impact. How did they use their time? How did they use their resources? Will the world be changed for the better because they sojourned through it? These are the things that ultimately matter in the end. It's about how we utilize our privileges to benefit those with far less than us.

The other perspective is to look at Jesus *historically* as a person with relatively little social privilege. From this perspective, Jesus was a poor Palestinian peasant, living in a location and time where he and his people were being oppressed by the Roman Empire. There was social unrest and upheaval, and there was little hope of rising above the circumstances of one's birth. Jesus was born a peasant and remained a peasant throughout his life. Other than his maleness and perhaps his Jewishness in some circumstances, he had very little social privilege that would benefit him. With this perspective in mind, we must again consider what it means that *he emptied himself.* Furthermore, we should consider what it means that he was "taking on the role of the slave, born in human form." How does a colonized peasant become a *slave?* And *why* would they ever willingly do that?

This is the tension that the way of Jesus calls us to grapple with—how do the most privileged of people *as well as* those with little privilege come together to empty themselves and to take on the form of a slave?

Historically, horrendous interpretations of this were used by oppressors as an excuse to keep folks in oppression. But this is not what Jesus did or what we're being called to do. Look at Jesus' earliest followers—his disciples were lower-class, poor peasants who found great hope and truth in the subversive message of Jesus. But Jesus' fundamental call was for them to begin living in light of a kingdom that they could not see and did not readily experience, through subversive, grassroots acts of generosity and service to others. Jesus himself was critiqued not only because he spent time with the marginalized of his society, but because he also made space for the most privileged, such as Jewish religious leaders and Roman officials. He didn't shy away from speaking truth to power—calling out their unjust behavior and ill intentions—but he also didn't shy away from *serving them* in their need as well.

Jesus, one who had very little in the way of social capital, gave what little he did have to help others—regardless of their identities or level of privilege. His willingness to give of himself even though he had so very little served as a powerful act of subversion of oppressive systems: he demonstrated that the way to true abundance and life comes not through domineering power but through relationships, serving, and loving others. This stood in stark contrast to the bombastic beliefs of Caesar and his officials that only through dominance and excessive wealth could true meaning and flourishing be achieved. By giving of himself, even for the good of his enemies, he broke through the hard hearts of the privileged and revealed to them a better way.

ACTIVISM AND ADVOCACY

How does self-emptying play out in our real world? In every situation of injustice, there are two paths of action necessary to create systemic, tangible change. These are the paths of *activism* and *advocacy*. The path of activism is for those willing to speak harsh truth to power, willing to put themselves on the line to demand that change is enacted. Activists will be on the front lines fighting until something changes. The path of advocacy is for those who are seeking to do "heart-work," reaching out to those in power and to regular people to help shift their hearts and minds through telling stories, educating, and equipping them with facts that can create a true and lasting inner shift. Oftentimes, activists feel that advocates are selling out and advocates feel that activists are hurting their cause—but the truth is, both are essential in any movement of social reform.

Regardless of our level of privilege and power, if we are to take seriously the kenotic way of Christ, we must be willing to engage in activism or advocacy—using whatever influence we have to create change, through either marching in the streets or cultivating deep conversations with those who see things differently than we do. Sometimes, we may be required to step outside our comfort zone and engage in a way that seems unnatural to us because it's what the moment demands of us as we seek to create a more just and equal world.

I am a natural advocate—I have a passion and a calling for building relationships with people who see the world differently than I do and seeking to change their perspective slowly but surely through genuine empathic understanding. I enjoy sitting across from people who see the world in a completely different way than I do and sharing my experience with them and theirs with me. But in recent years, as Black people were being brutally murdered by police officers across the country, many of my clergy colleagues and I were called out of our comfort zone of advocacy and into full-on activism.

For us, this meant putting on our clergy collars and heading to the small town of La Mesa, California, where a young Black man named Aumarie Johnson had been arrested while waiting for his friends at a bus stop. In response to this example of blatant racism by the police department, protests broke out around the police department headquarters, and the police immediately began arresting, teargassing, and physically assaulting the protesters. Local Black Lives Matter coalitions put out a call for white people to come and put their bodies on the line to protect Black and Brown individuals—knowing that white people were much less likely to face the severe consequences that Black and Brown individuals might.

When we parked our car and walked toward La Mesa's police station, I was terrified. I could hear the police shooting beanbags and tear gas into a crowd of maybe a thousand protesters, and the screams and cries of those who had been hit. I heard the chants ringing above the chaos, "I can't breathe!" and "Say her name—Breonna Taylor!" I didn't *want* to be in the midst of this turmoil. I didn't *need* to be here. My privilege afforded me the opportunity to sit safely at home. But my faith *demanded* that I do something. Let me be clear, I don't believe for a second that it was "virtuous" for me and my white clergy colleagues to show up for the protests. We didn't do it because we wanted to feel good about ourselves. We did it because we knew that if folks like us didn't take seriously the concerns of our Black and Brown neighbors, things were only going to get worse.

We *needed* to use our privilege—our very bodies, in this case—in order to protect and advance the agenda of the protesters. And so we did. Throughout the night, we stood in the midst of protesters, chanting with them, encouraging them, recording them, and being visible to police to try to deter them from taking extreme actions. We breathed an ungodly amount of tear gas and nearly got trampled on numerous times as we stood with young protesters whose every chant was filled with a palpable mix of anguish and fury. They were living in a nation that was set up against them. There was nothing they could do, nowhere they could go where they would be safe. They lived in a constant state of fear. How could they *not* be angry? But an even more unsettling question emerged for me during the protest: How had I remained uninvolved for so long?

There is simply no way one can take seriously the life and teachings of Jesus and not be compelled to act whenever injustice emerges. The Hebrew Bible, again and again, declares that the worship that God desires is "to do justice, and to love kindness, and to walk humbly with your God" (Mic. 6:8). Yet the faith that I inherited had very little emphasis on justice. Instead, we focused on believing the right things, converting others to our worldview, and seeking God's blessing upon our comfortable, privileged lives.

For so many, Christianity is really nothing more than a self-help program or intellectual pursuit. But the movement that Jesus began is primarily concerned with working alongside God to bring about redemption to the world through one subversive act of love at a time. Kenosis, or self-emptying, is one of the clearest examples of what Christlike love looks like: being willing to own the ways that we have been blessed and privileged and asking, "How can this be leveraged for the good of another?"

SUBVERTING SLAVERY

All through the New Testament we see the language of slavery seemingly glorified. Whenever we hear the word "slavery" in our modern context, we think back to the grave sin of slavery that the United States is built upon, and we are rightfully left feeling rather uncomfortable by a positive usage of the term in our holy texts. The Greek word used in Philippians 2 and in other writings of the apostle Paul is *doulou,* which has two primary meanings: "slave," with the oppressive understanding mentioned previously, as well as "servant." The same Greek word is the root of the English term "doula," or midwife, someone who helps another through the process of giving birth. Somewhere in the tension between these three definitions of *doulou* lies tremendous wisdom for the posture of disciples of Christ.

In a very true sense, Jesus lived in a world where he and his people were slaves. The Jewish people had a long history of being taken captive and enslaved by oppressive empires, experiences that lived in their collective memory. From a theological lens, Christians assert that God chose to incarnate as a first-century Jewish man, as a member of a community that constantly lived under the threat of colonizing forces moving in, yet again, to oppress and exploit them. This is a theological insight that must not be taken lightly. The creator of the universe chooses to not only stand in solidarity with, but to physically become a member of one of the most oppressed communities in history. God doesn't merely reach out to comfort them but chooses to kneel down in the dust and dirt, the muck and mire, and become one of them. The God of the oppressed becomes one of the oppressed. God in Christ makes clear whose side God is on when it comes of questions of injustice.

This also suggests that in conversations about privilege, our assumption should be that God is on the side of all of those with the least privilege or power. This runs contrary to the dominant religious narratives that permeate human history—how often do we attribute military victory, colonization, and power to God's blessing? We assume that if our people come out on top, if we are victorious in our conquest, that this must be a sign of God's favor. This is one reason, I believe, that Jesus was so offensive in his day and why the image of Jesus the slave was quickly abandoned in the early days of the Christian movement for that of an imperial conqueror, as we see in the book of Revelation.

All of the disciples and all of the religious leaders who surrounded Jesus during his earthly ministry were deeply confused—how could this man be the long-awaited messiah? The messianic figure in Judaism was one who came with power and might, the ability to conquer the conquerors and establish a new kingdom where the oppressive empire once stood. This vision is clearly illustrated in the prophecies of the Hebrew Bible, like this text from the book of Isaiah:

Every warrior's boot used in battle
and every garment rolled in blood
will be destined for burning,
will be fuel for the fire.
For to us a child is born,
to us a son is given,
and the government will be on his shoulders.
And he will be called
Wonderful Counselor, Mighty God,
Everlasting Father, Prince of Peace.
Of the greatness of his government and peace
there will be no end.
He will reign on David's throne
and over his kingdom,
establishing and upholding it
with justice and righteousness
from that time on and forever.

(Isa. 9:5–7 NIV)

This prophecy clearly indicates a messiah who will come not as a slave, but as a conqueror who will overthrow unjust empires and establish a new government of justice and righteousness that will exist throughout all time. It is understandable that many Jews in the first century looked at Jesus and his motley band of disciples and scoffed—this man wasn't anything like the messiah that was promised by Isaiah. Not only was the government not upon his shoulders, but Caesar's government ultimately executed him. And the peace he brought? There wasn't much of it. Within forty years of his crucifixion, the entire city of Jerusalem and the holy temple was burnt to the ground. Jesus didn't (and still doesn't) look like the Messiah everyone was expecting.

Herein lies the subversive power of the kenotic way: Jesus demonstrates that worldly power is not necessary to transform the world. One doesn't need political might, status, or wealth to overturn injustice. Despite everything we've been conditioned to believe, Jesus shows us that the biggest threat to oppressive systems is individuals who opt out of the oppressor's game. This is what it means that God in Christ becomes a "slave," a member of an oppressed people, as God's method of redeeming the world. Again, from a theological perspective, God willingly gives up all power and privilege that comes with being God in order to become an oppressed minority, and from that lowly position manages to subversively transform the world.

COMMUNITY ORGANIZING LIKE JESUS

Jesus demonstrates a method of activism and community organizing that is not often understood by well-intentioned privileged people (myself included). Effective organizing doesn't require that we work to get the powerful and privileged to understand our perspective and make changes on our behalf. No, effective organizing begins with a group of oppressed people deciding, as best they can, to opt out of living in the system of oppression. In my work as an LGBTQ+ Christian activist, this has looked like working with LGBTQ+ people of faith to create our own churches, conferences, and retreats outside of "traditional" churches. We decided that we didn't need to wait for our denominations to accept us, but rather, we could form new spaces and live out our faith without affirmation from systems of oppressive power.

Now, of course, one cannot *completely* opt out of systemic oppression simply by choosing to do so. Jesus still faced constraints, discrimination, and persecution throughout his life and ministry. But the basis for his life was God's economy and governance and not that of Rome. He believed that God would provide for him—his food, his clothing, his protection, his power—and he sought to convince his people to believe the same thing for themselves. Thus they began to live in an alternative society, a reality beyond the control of the empire, which gradually drained the empire of the power it had over them.

When Jesus' disciples came together and began living in an alternative reality—one where they opted out of the economic, political, and social systems of the empire and began to create their own—this is when the powers that be began to worry. As others looked at the Christians and saw that their reality was, in many ways, far better than that afforded them by the oppressive empire, more and more began to convert, not primarily because they believed theological claims, but because they experienced a new way of seeing and being in the world—a new kingdom, if you will. This became a real problem when even members of the imperial government began to hear of this new way of living and willingly converted—like Cornelius the centurion and his household in Acts 10.

The proclamation of the lordship of Jesus by the early apostles was not primarily a proclamation of how to escape postmortem hell and enter heaven, but rather, how to escape the hell that *everyone* lives within a culture of dominance, oppression, and greed. This message appealed not just to the oppressed peoples, but also to those within the hierarchy of oppression. For systems of privilege to operate, they require belief in a collective narrative. Rome had the narratives of Aeneas and of Romulus and Remus, describing its divine origins, that were taught to the children of the empire from an early age. America has its own founding mythology about the valiant pilgrims leaving the oppression of the British crown and being led on a divine conquest to a New World and establishing a "city upon a hill," a holy beacon of freedom for all of humanity. Neither one of these myths is *true,* but very few people ever think to question their veracity. Instead, we learn them, we teach them, and we celebrate them, and in doing so, we deepen our commitment to oppression.

The "myth" that Jesus and the early Christians proclaimed revealed the lies embedded in the myths that upheld the Roman Empire—that true power was found not in conquering, but in serving. That the key to satisfaction was not wealth, but sharing with one another. Most people in their day and in ours believed these statements at some very basic level, but very few ever tried to embody them. This is what made Jesus so revolutionary—he practiced what he preached. He showed us how, through opting out of the operating systems of the day, we could begin to create a new world right in the midst of this one. In this new world, one's education, ethnicity, status, sexuality, disability, gender, or class didn't matter. One could be a Samaritan woman, a eunuch, a Roman official, or a leper, and experience the same level of provision and embrace in the new community that was being created.

But to experience this new reality, there was a sacrifice involved: one needed to "take up the cross," literally meaning to give up one's faith in the ways of the empire and to begin living outside of its most fundamental expectations and requirements. Jesus instructed his followers to fulfill their basic obligations as citizens—render unto Caesar—but also not to rely on the mechanism of the empire for anything that they needed. Instead, they were to "seek first the kingdom of God," to trust in their Creator and in the beloved community forming around God's promises. They opted out of even the most basic provisions of the empire. Rome had an advanced welfare system for its era, which provided *tesserae frumentariae,* basic bread rations for poor citizens, in many of the major cities throughout the empire—excluding most colonized nations. Jesus taught his followers not to rely on Rome for their bread, but rather to pray to God for their daily bread ration. By creating a subversive society within a society, Jesus was empowering those with little privilege as well as those with much to opt out of the corrupt systems of the empire and begin participating in a new empire that was *always* present and accessible, if only they had the faith to perceive it.

Jesus became a *slave* to show those with no power and privilege and those with much that the true path to the world that the Jewish people prayed for and that the Roman Empire sought to establish through force was accessed through *self-emptying, sacrificial service.* He invited his followers to become doulas, or midwives, of a new world, amid the one that they were living in. It didn't require them to rise through the ranks of power and privilege; it didn't require them to obtain great wealth or to organize a mighty army. Instead, it required them to renounce their belief in the myths that they had been conditioned to believe from an early age and begin believing a new story—one in which the least are understood to be the greatest, where the poor are seen to be the wealthiest, and those who are maligned by the powerful are seen to be truly blessed. It is one thing to mentally assent to these claims, but another thing to begin living them out. It's risky. It feels dangerous and irresponsible. But the promise of Jesus is that those who do will experience provision and abundance. They will gain so much more through their willingness to sacrifice.

TRANSFORMING POLITICAL SYSTEMS

This call has been interpreted many ways by many people throughout the centuries—is this a call to disengage from government and society altogether and form new self-sustaining communities? Many have sought to do just that, with little long-term success. Instead of disengagement, I believe that the intention of Jesus and the early Christians was to transform the systems of the world through tangible actions. As more people converted to the way of Jesus and turned their back on the ways of empire, it would gradually become harder for the empire to enforce oppressive policies and practices. One could argue that Jesus was using a fundamental principle of democracy—if enough people not only demand a new way of being in the world but begin to participate in that way of being, they *force* the government to change.

You see, Jesus showed that there is true power in community organizing. How could this peasant rabbi from Nazareth pose any true threat to the empire or even the religious establishment? And yet, they feared him, and ultimately executed him based on that fear. Why? Because he had tremendous power through being able to inspire and organize regular people to begin living in a different way. The power, for Jesus, was in the masses of people who began to follow him. The masses of people who began to truly believe that a new world was possible and that they could create it, here and now. Caesar had a mighty army and great wealth, but if entire sectors of the empire simply chose to no longer participate in the system of power because they truly believed that they would be provided for by God and could create a better world, what good would Caesar's army or money be? The confidence of oppressors lies in their belief that people dislike change and grow comfortable in their oppression. Jesus' vision of a new world shook people out of their comfort and demanded that they make an immediate change in their lives. That was *literally* what the word "gospel" meant, a proclamation of political or military victory. And this was the content of the message that he preached:

> Jesus came to Galilee, proclaiming the good news of God, and saying, "The time is fulfilled, and the kingdom of God has come near; repent, and believe in the good news." (Mark 1:14–15)

Jesus declared that a new kingdom was emerging in the world through his teachings, and he called all people to take immediate action: repent, meaning change the way they were living, and believe that this new kingdom was a reality and a possibility.

This call of Jesus has echoed through the ages, and today it reverberates within each one of us: the conviction that there is another way to organize our lives and world. Most of us believe it on an intellectual level. Most of us are happy to post on Facebook about what the world *should* be like. Most of us are probably even willing to show up at a protest or rally demanding change. But this is not what is required of us. If we claim to follow Jesus, and if we really believe his message and example are the keys to transforming the world, we must actually be willing to shake things up. To willingly sacrifice our privilege, power, comfort, and wealth, to create a more just and equal world. The self-emptying was at the heart of this earliest creed of the Christians, following in Jesus' own example of giving up his position to become like us—a human, a servant, and a midwife of a more beautiful world.

DISCUSSION QUESTIONS

1. What do you imagine it was like for Jesus to have privilege and power on a divine scale, but have little power or privilege in his earthly social context? How does that paradox shape your faith?
2. What does it mean to you that Jesus did not just pour himself out for others but *emptied* himself? What would it mean for us to do the same?
3. Do you feel more wired for activism or advocacy? What are some tangible ways you can lean into that wiring to leverage your privilege for the common good?
4. Does your faith community have a regular advocacy component? What issues could your faith community help to raise in the public square of your community?
5. The author outlines the social and political teachings of Jesus. How do you feel about this understanding of Jesus' ministry? How does it square with your own faith and understanding of Jesus?
6. What would it look like for earthly powers to be subverted by the power of servanthood? What would it mean for you to take "the form of a slave"?

Chapter 6

OBEDIENCE UNTO DEATH

Being found in human form he humbled himself by becoming obedient as far as death, even the worst kind of death—death that comes through a cross.

—Philippians 2:7b–8, au. trans.

One of the off-putting things that many spiritual seekers run into when exploring the world's great spiritual traditions is the language of *death*. Of course, it is the fear of death that drives many people to begin their spiritual search, and many are surprised to find that in many religious texts, not only is death not feared, but reflecting on it is encouraged. When you think about it, this makes perfect sense. The best way to overcome a fear is to confront it directly—to stare it in the face and to choose to walk through it. This is certainly true with Christianity: death is literally at the core of everything we believe and do. The central ritual of Christians—the Eucharist—recalls the death of Jesus, reminds us of the great sacrifice that was made on our behalf, and calls us to embody the same sacrifice in our daily life.

Jesus himself often called his followers to a radical way of living whereby they are always willing to die: "If any want to become my followers, let them deny themselves and take up their cross and follow me. For those who want to save their life will lose it, and those who lose their life for my sake will find it" (Matt. 16:24–25). Throughout the ages, theologians have interpreted these words in a wide variety of ways. The most common is to understand these extreme words metaphorically, calling us to live in a sacrificial and selfless way for God and for others. There is truth to this interpretation—I've already suggested that this is one of the most fundamental postures of Christian living. But for a moment, let's set aside our religious understanding of Jesus and look at him strictly from a historical standpoint, seeing Jesus as the political revolutionary (or zealot) that he was.[1]

Jesus lived in an unjust society and throughout his life witnessed the constant abuse of his people by the Roman Empire. Not only this, but his religious tradition consistently reminded him of how often the Jewish people had been enslaved by cruel empires such as Babylon and Egypt. This bleak reality is what fueled the messianic hope within the Jewish religion—an oppressed people longed for someone to liberate them from the hellish reality they often experienced and allow them to live in peace. So Jesus, like many other young religious Jews of his day, was inspired to seek to bring about liberation for his people. Many other would-be messiahs sought to liberate the Jewish people by force, organizing mass rebellion. Time and time again, these efforts failed—it was nearly impossible to fight against the most powerful empire the world had ever seen.

Jesus, on the other hand, sought a different kind of revolution. His was a social revolution, one that usurped the power of the oppressor through choosing to live in an alternative social order right under their noses. If Jesus could win over the masses to living in his new reality, called the kingdom of God, whereby they cared for and provided for one another, trusting in the provision and protection of God, Rome's power would be rendered moot. Jesus' vision of subversion was subtle; he called his people to continue to participate in the requirements of the empire— "render to Caesar the things that are Caesar's" (Mark 12:17

KJV)—while simultaneously living within the economy of God. Eventually, as more people began to live according to this way, Rome would find itself with little means of control over the Jewish people. The empire would literally be defeated through the power of love, compassion, and faith.

But as idyllic as this sounds, Jesus knew full well that inspiring any revolutionary effort would likely get him killed. At the heart of the matter was a question of worship. The Roman Empire was so effective in part because of its psychological and spiritual demands on the peoples it colonized. Every subject of the empire was required to worship the emperor as a god. Across every Roman colony one would see buildings and coins declaring "Caesar is Lord." Roman officials would hail Caesar as the "son of god" and declare him the "savior of the world." The Jewish tradition had long stood opposed to any such demands by any colonizing empire—the Hebrew Bible recounts numerous stories of faithful heroes who refused to bow to narcissistic kings, reserving their reverence for God alone. Jesus followed in this tradition—worship was due to God alone, and a crucial part of the new kingdom he sought to inaugurate was honoring the true Lord and God of all creation.

Not only did this message cause offense to the empire, but it was just as offensive to the Jewish religious establishment in Jerusalem. Jesus stood in the tradition of Jewish reformists, calling people away from rigid obedience to the rules and rituals of their faith that often became the primary focus, to a more basic understanding of what it meant to be faithful through living a just and humble life. Jesus was deeply critical of what the chief priests were allowing to happen in the temple in Jerusalem, which is what led him to dramatically overturn tables in the temple complex, nearly inciting a riot. He consistently found himself at odds with many religious leaders in Jerusalem, calling them "whitewashed tombs" and "a den of thieves"—the idea being that they displayed an outward sense of piety while internally being no different from the imperial forces who exploited them.

Jesus' message of a new kingdom emerging in the midst of his world, one that established a social order outside of the Roman Empire and a spiritual order outside of the religious establishment, was clearly a dangerous one, regardless of how peaceful or nonviolent it may have been. It gave hope to a weary people that they could experience a new way of living that was marked by freedom and peace— and such hope is the fundamental fuel for revolutionary action. Thus when Jesus called his followers to "take up their cross" and to be willing to "lose their life," he was being quite literal. Once this revolutionary way of seeing and being was discovered by the powers that be, he knew that they would revert to their one reliable strategy—violence.

THE GOD WHO DIES

Now when we switch back to the lens of the Jesus of faith described in the Kenosis Hymn, a new level of theological significance arises. Paul writes, "Being found in human form he humbled himself by becoming obedient as far as death, even the worst kind of death—death that comes through a cross" (Phil. 2:7b–8, au. trans.). Not only does God step out of the role of ultimate privilege and power to stand in solidarity with humanity in our brokenness, not only does the Creator willingly become a servant to the creation, but we are told that God, immortal creator of life and death, willingly submits to death of the cruelest kind—

capital punishment. In the spectrum of privilege, we have watched Jesus go from the absolute most privileged position to the absolute least privileged position, from King of Kings to executed felon.

The one we believe to be the incarnation of God willingly allows himself to be murdered by the very beings God created, as a display of love and as a mirror to show just how broken humanity had become. On the cross, Jesus is killed for proclaiming a gospel of grace, inclusion, and liberation. On the cross, those who watched Jesus and his peaceful revolution see in a moment the stunning contrast between God's desire for the world and the corrupt ways of the empire. Jesus' death is a most complex picture of breathtaking love and unimaginable depravity. Jesus had done nothing morally wrong—everyone knew that. He simply gave hope to a hopeless people and inspired them to live out the values of their faith more tangibly through subversive acts of love. Yet the righteousness of this way of being shed light on the corruption and wickedness of the powers at work in society, and therefore could not be left unpunished. Thus the Christian story culminates with a cross.

At the moment of crucifixion, God in Christ stands in solidarity with both the falsely accused and the most wicked humans on earth. No one lacks privilege more than an inmate on death row, who has had *every* right stripped away, even the right to live. In our day, as in Jesus', many of those on death row are there because they have been falsely accused, often based, in some part, on their race or ethnicity. There is no injustice worse than being sentenced to death for crimes you did not commit, based on prejudice and bias against you. Yet this is where we find Jesus both then and now. In the kenotic descent of Christ, this is rock bottom. From God, to human, to slave, to criminal—God in Christ fully and finally rids himself of any semblance of privilege and power. What may be more stunning is that not only does Christ do this, but he calls us to do the same.

The path of death demonstrated in the kenosis of Christ is both a tangible death and a spiritual one. It's a willingness to put one's life on the line, even in unjust circumstances, in the defense of others. But for one to be willing to take such a drastic action in the world, a profound spiritual death must first occur. Many traditions would call this the death of the ego or the part of ourselves that we project into the world that doesn't represent our truest self at our core. The image of God in Christ emptying himself through gradually giving up all of the privilege and identification with his external identities is a profound image for the spiritual path we must all walk if we seek to live in union with God.

The mystic author Cynthia Bourgeault has written profoundly and yet succinctly about the unique spiritual path that Jesus embodies through his kenosis. In her book *The Wisdom Jesus*, she writes:

> Underlying all of Jesus' teaching is a clarion call to a radical shift in consciousness: away from the alienation and polarization of the egoic operating system and into the unified field of divine abundance that can be perceived only through the heart. . . . In whatever life circumstance, Jesus always responded with the same motion of self-emptying—or to put it another way, the same motion of descent: going lower, taking the lower place, not the higher.[2]

Bourgeault suggests that, in contrast to many of the world's spiritual traditions that perceive the way to union with God through ascent, Jesus reveals a stunningly different way: going lower. If we are to experience the kind of abundant life that Jesus speaks of, the path isn't through reaching for our highest selves but rather through a reckless emptying of ourselves. We must be willing to walk through those moments of our lives where a death of our ego occurs with an awareness that therein lies not only the key to our own spiritual awakening, but also the key to creating a more just and generous world.

EGO DEATH

I am an Enneagram Three, the type Richard Rohr has said are emblematic of American ambition.[3] Threes are known to be ego-driven individuals, people who seek to find love and validation through high public performance and the external affirmation that comes from it. So when Threes experience a moment of ego death, it is experienced much more acutely than for other personality types. Recently, I transitioned from serving as the lead pastor of an incredible church community, and that experience was one of painful but generative ego death. Since my teenage years, my identity has been wrapped up in being a pastor—everything in my life was aimed at achieving that goal and living into that calling. But after reaching that goal and becoming the lead pastor of a church at the age of twenty-five, I slowly began to question if this role was what I was *called* to live into.

Over the course of my nearly four-year tenure, I learned a ton and experienced a lot of public "success." But internally, I was wrestling deeply with my own spirituality and my personal desires for my life. While pastoring for nearly a year during the COVID-19 pandemic, I spent a lot of time reassessing the trajectory of my life and the choices I was making both personally and professionally. During this time, I came to a painful conclusion: serving as a full-time parish pastor was not where I desired to be for this season of my life. Yet the entirety of my identity was tied up in being Pastor Brandan. In work as well as in my personal life, my self-understanding was and had always been as a pastor, albeit a very unconventional one. This realization led me to have difficult conversations with my community's leaders and eventually make the choice to transition out of congregational ministry and into a new season of my personal and professional life.

On the surface, this experience may not seem all that difficult to the average reader. But anyone who has ever gone through a crisis of identity—vocational or otherwise—will know just how painful these moments can be. Reassessing who we are, what our life is all about, is one of the scariest journeys we can walk. (This is precisely why we've developed language like "quarterlife crisis" and "midlife crisis.") As Father Richard Rohr has taught, the first half of life is generally driven by our ego desires—asserting who we believe ourselves to be, competition, and achievement.[4] This stage is crucial to being a functioning human in the world—we have to understand who we are, and we have to establish a trajectory for our lives to work within. The problem is that most Western societies have elevated this half of life to be the *whole* of our lives. We so value ego, competition, and success that anything that pulls us away from these innate drives is often demonized.

But the second half of life, according to Rohr, is where true inner kenosis happens for many people—it's a process of understanding and appreciating our egoic identity, but not fundamentally identifying with it. We are no longer "the pastor," "the teacher," "the star athlete," but rather, we begin to contemplate how those aspects of our identity can become tools not only for our own fulfillment but in service of the world. We recognize that our identities and accomplishments alone do not actually have the power to fulfill us, and we begin to lean into those things that do. This is a very real, very painful dying process. Brené Brown sums it up so poignantly:

> Midlife is not about the fear of death. Midlife *is* death. Tearing down the walls that we spent our entire life building is death. Like it or not, at some point during midlife, you're going down, and after that, there are only two choices: staying down or enduring rebirth.[5]

This is where the narrative of Jesus is so psychologically and spiritually helpful: the suffering, death, and resurrection of Jesus is a profound metaphor for this process of ego death. As Jesus is arrested, tried, tortured, and murdered, we get a sense of what a painful process it can be to willingly enter the process of maturation and spiritual evolution. Oftentimes, these processes don't occur willfully for us—instead we are thrust into painful moments of crisis and failure where we must reckon with what is truly real and what is most meaningful to us. Is the career, the title, the money worth it? If we believe that it is, we may well be confronted with a circumstance that dramatically strips it from us, throwing us into an existential crisis. Or perhaps we will have a moment of awakening where we begin to ask critical questions about how we're living our lives, and more gently but usually no less painfully begin to grapple with the answers.

However we enter into this process and whenever it occurs in our lives (it usually happens many times), ego deaths are a painful but essential part of the spiritual journey. They require a kenotic descent—an emptying of our "false self" to discover what is truest about us. And what is truest about us is not our privilege, our power, or our success. What is truest about us is our interconnectivity to God and to everyone else, the realization of nonduality, that there is not "us" and "them," but that in God we *all* live and move and have our being, and therefore, we are essentially one. What is good for the other is good for us, and vice versa. Only in this space do we begin to find the ability to be reckless enough to give of our privilege in service of others.

Only after an experience of ego death do we experience resurrection to a meaningful life. Only after coming to terms with all the false promises of our privilege and power do we face the pivotal choice to either stay down, clinging to those identities once considered fundamental, seeking to exploit them for the little power they have left, or to accept a new reality of service and grace. To conserve or to progress.

This is the goal of the kenotic path. It is one that requires inner spiritual work that fuels outward actions to create a more whole and holy world for all. But unlike so many other traditions, the Christian spiritual path is not one that calls for us to aim high, to reach for an unattainable and exalted divine status, but rather to go down low, recklessly giving up every ounce of privilege without a second thought. Cynthia Bourgeault writes, "In our voluntary relinquishing of our most cherished possessions, we make manifest what love really looks like."[6] What is more cherished than our egoic identity? It alone is the channel through which we lay hold of positions of power, wealth, influence, and authority. If we are to embody the way of Jesus, we must be willing to relinquish these possessions, first within ourselves, and then to the world around us. The way of Jesus isn't one of conservation or even ascetic renunciation—it's the path of radical, sacrificial squandering of any privilege we may have inadvertently inherited by our birth. As the Sufi mystic Rumi wrote, "Love gambles away every gift God bestows."[7]

This reckless, subversive relinquishing requires faith and trust in God's goodness and love; it requires a dying to the ego and a rising again to a realization of fundamental oneness. Whether we intentionally pursue this path of death or life thrusts it upon us without our consent, each of us will come face-to-face with the moment of ego death, and our response in that moment will determine the trajectory of our lives and of the world around us.

LOVE IS NOT "FAIR"

The kenotic path of Jesus can be interpreted in many ways, but when viewed through the lens of the cross, it becomes clear that our notions of fairness are turned on their heads in light of Jesus' sacrifice. Christian theology has long held that Jesus didn't *have* to go to the cross. The passion narrative in the Gospel of John has Pontius Pilate declaring to the crowds demanding Jesus' death, "I find no fault in him" (John 19:4 KJV). Reading the passion narrative not as a literal record of history but instead as a metaphor (as it's used in the Kenosis Hymn), Jesus willingly subjects himself to death because he *knows* that on the other side of such a sacrifice is the promise of new life.

When we think about kenosis in relation to our privilege and power, it can often feel unfair. It seems that God is requiring that we willingly give up our head start in life,

which has benefited us greatly, but that we also didn't willingly pursue. You may think, "I didn't choose to be born
white, male, heterosexual, or able-bodied," so why would
you be *required* to give up those things for the good of
those who lack privilege? Throughout Jesus' ministry, he
often was accused of being unfair. There were those who,
according to religious standards, were sanctified and pure,
but those were not the people Jesus often extended blessing to. Instead, he offered blessings to those who might
be considered sinful, lazy, unrighteous, unrepentant, and
of ill repute. In the Gospel stories, Jesus uses his privilege
and power not for his own benefit, but for the benefit of
those who need it the most, trusting that even as he gave so
freely, God would provide everything that he needed with
an equal measure of liberality.

One of the primary roadblocks to people following
Jesus is precisely in their perception of "fairness." So much
theology has emerged in our consumeristic, capitalistic
society that claims that financial stability, good health, and
upward mobility is a sign of God's blessing, and that those
who do not have access to such favor are somehow lacking the blessing of the Almighty. When this is the paradigm,
asking folks to give *everything* they have been "blessed"
with for the good of those who haven't been "blessed"
and even perhaps may be seen as "cursed" seems radically
unfair.

Remember the story of a young Jewish scholar who
approaches Jesus and asks him, "What must I do to inherit
eternal life?" (Matt. 19:16, au. trans.). This young man
goes out of his way to explain to Jesus that he has been faithful to the commandments and has been materially blessed
by God. Surely, his faithfulness and blessing are a sign that
he is on the right path toward eternal life.

Jesus looks at this eager and oblivious young man with pity and says, "My son, there is still one thing that you are lacking. Sell everything you have and give it to those in poverty—then you will inherit eternal life." I love what the next verse says about the young man's response to Jesus, primarily because it's so authentically human: "When the young man heard this, he went away sad, because he had great wealth" (Matt. 19:22 NIV). This young man is saddened by Jesus' request to give up everything he had for those who had not—and would this not be our response as well? I mean, why haven't you sold everything and given it away? If you claim to be a follower of Jesus, this command seems straightforward and clear. Yet here both you and I sit, with savings accounts, abundant possessions, and a voice in our heads seeking to justify our disobedience.

Jesus' response to the young man was not calling him to live an ascetic life—no, instead, it was calling him to embrace the path of death, with full faith that if he lives a life of generosity, he too will be provided for. After all, Jesus taught, "Give, and it will be given to you" (Luke 6:38a). I don't believe that this is some sort of magical or even supernatural equation—instead, it's a simple fact that when we are recklessly generous with our blessings, we will often attract "blessing" into our own lives. It may not feel fair to be required to give what we have earned or inherited to others, but equality usually doesn't *feel* fair to those who are on top. When the mountains are lowered and the valleys are exalted, those on the mountaintop often feel as if they're losing out—because they are. They are losing some privileged access. They are losing some decision-making power. They are losing a surplus of resources.

But a mind that has been reborn through death understands that we're all fundamentally one, and that when we give of our own privilege and power, it is not truly leaving us, but is instead spreading out among the one new humanity that God is seeking to create, ensuring that everyone has all that they need and can flourish. It is through the process of utter and absolute death to our privilege, first within ourselves and then in the actual world, through an absolute willingness to squander what we have for the good of others, that we truly model the kenotic way of Christ.

DISCUSSION QUESTIONS

1. Is death a frightening concept for you? Setting aside the idea of an afterlife in heaven, what does death mean to you as a Christian, both literally and metaphorically?
2. How do you feel about the idea of reckless self-sacrifice? What would it look like for you to "deny yourself" and "take up your cross"?
3. Does it make a difference to you that Jesus not only died, but that he was killed through capital punishment by an unjust empire? Why or why not?
4. In what ways have you experienced an ego death along your journey thus far? What are some spiritual practices that have helped you with "dying to self" and rising to your true self?
5. What do you think of Rohr and Brown's take on the midlife experience? Does it ring true for your experience or that of anyone you know?
6. Read Matthew 19:16–22 and 20:1–16. How do you respond to the idea that God is not fair?

Chapter 7

A NEW KIND OF POWER

For this reason, God has greatly exalted him and gave him the name that is above every other name, so that at the name of Jesus, every knee will bend—of all beings in the universe—and every tongue will gladly confess that Jesus Christ is Lord, to the glory of God the Father.
—Philippians 2:9–11, au. trans.

Whenever we think about justice and equity, power inevitably comes into play. Whoever holds the positions or means of power holds the ability to either use it to establish said justice or abuse it for their own benefit. As we've seen thus far in the Kenosis Hymn, the way of Jesus is to recognize the power that is given, but then to recklessly surrender it to the powerless, the marginalized, and those who have been downtrodden. But there is yet another subversive twist to the kenotic way of seeing and being in the world—once we can acknowledge our privilege and power and utilize it for the good of others, the hymn suggests that we then receive a new kind of power, a true kind of power, that comes directly from God.

In verse 9, the hymn changes direction completely. The trajectory has been a downward one—God in Christ is willingly surrendering and sacrificing his identity and the power that comes with it to help defend, heal, and empower others. Suddenly, there is a change in direction from humiliation to exaltation: "For this reason, God has greatly exalted him." The exaltation of Jesus is seemingly dependent on his willingness to empty himself of his privilege and power for the sake of love. Theologically, one might believe that this statement is unique to Jesus alone, that he alone is bestowed power from God because of his selfless way of being. But remember that the context of this hymn is *instructive*—we have been told to *adopt this mindset* and thus one could expect that in some way, when we align our lives with this way of being in the world, we too will tap into this divine sense of power or exaltation as well.

Let me be clear that I am not suggesting that we become equal to Christ or receive some sort of supernatural reward for following Jesus—those theological conversations seem frankly irrelevant when one studies the life and teachings of Jesus. Jesus came with a clear mission to transform this world here and now and was not very focused on what was to happen in "the world to come." Peter himself tries to get Jesus to focus on what would happen to him in the afterlife, how he might be exalted because of his faithful obedience to Jesus. Jesus responds with a bit of cryptic messianic language that culminates in these words: "But many who are first will be last, and many who are last will be first" (Matt. 19:30 NIV). His message is clear—those who become servants in this life will be blessed both now and in the world to come. Those who exploit and abuse power in this life will be less in the world to come. (Notice he *doesn't* say eternally condemned, rather, just put in last place.)

Jesus promised that if we lived according to his radically subversive path that it would benefit the world we're living in here and now, and into eternity. He taught that our actions in this life have a lasting impact on the future—perhaps even an eternal impact. This perspective helps to raise the stakes for us, regardless of what we believe happens after death. The point is that in our interconnected universe, our individual decisions, mindsets, and actions have a measurable impact that ripples out far beyond our time, place, and conscious sphere of influence. And the Kenosis Hymn suggests that Jesus' willingness to surrender his power and privilege in service of those with little power and privilege resulted in a sense of exaltation.

A NEW KIND OF LORD

It's hard not to see both messianic language as well as Roman imperial language in this section. In both the Jewish understanding of what the messiah would do and the Roman understanding of who the emperor was, there was a common belief that through brute, physical force, infused with divine power, these leaders would conquer and establish an eternal kingdom. The expectation was that justice was going to be accomplished through destroying their enemies and that the divine human who accomplished this should be declared the rightful king and lord. In fact, throughout the Greco-Roman world, coins and government buildings were engraved with the proclamation *Kaiser Kyrios,* which literally means "Caesar the Lord," an affirmation of the divine place that these powerful rulers held in the hearts and minds of Roman citizens.[1]

When the early Christians began proclaiming *Kyrios Iēsous Christos,* meaning "Jesus Christ is Lord," they were implicitly claiming that they did not believe the central claim of the Roman Empire—that Caesar was the divinely sent ruler of the world. The combination of *Kyrios* and *Christos* was also a claim to Jews who surrounded the early

Christians, declaring that Jesus was, in fact, the "Christ," the Hellenized word for "messiah." This claim was at once laughable and offensive to both groups—the Jewish peasant who was executed by the state is the *true Caesar* and *true messiah*? You can imagine how ridiculous this sounded—especially when the early Christians went on about Jesus being alive after everyone witnessed him die. This proclamation was not only ridiculous; it was also illegal. Allegiance to Caesar was the most basic commitment one was required to make under Roman imperial rule. In fact, our religious language of "sacrament" comes from Roman imperial language for the pledge of allegiance to the Lord Caesar that soldiers in the Roman army were required to make. Scholar R. Alan Streett writes:

> Tacitus (56–117 CE), the Roman senator and historian, referred to *sacramentum* during the Empire as the verbal pledge of allegiance a soldier gives to his emperor. Tacitus was the first to speak of "receiving the sacrament" (*sacramentum acciperent*) because the oath was being administered to the soldier on behalf of the emperor.[2]

You can see just how intimately politics was tied to the early Christian understanding of the way of Jesus. The phrase "Jesus is Lord" was not primarily a theological affirmation but rather a sociopolitical declaration that one's allegiance did not lie with the government or religious establishment, but in the radical social vision of the revolutionary Jesus. In one's decision to follow this Lord, one committed to resisting the way of exploitation—giving up privilege for the good of others—but in a radically subversive sense one also was laying claim to a deeper power, one that actually had the ability to threaten all of the oppressive systems and structures in a profoundly real way.

The early church was not primarily a religious gathering, but a social movement where individuals opted out of participation in the dominant society and began constructing a new social ordering within their own little community. It was as if they were realizing Jesus' vision of the kingdom of God on earth as in heaven on a micro scale, with the hope that the more people who joined, the more communities would form, and one day they would wake up and see a world transformed not by force but through sacrificial love and devotion to the way of Jesus.

Now of course things didn't work out so well—within a few hundred years after Jesus' crucifixion, this subversive religiopolitical movement had been co-opted by the empire, seriously diluting the true power of Jesus' followers, and replacing it with the power and privilege of empire. On one hand, this was a brilliant strategy of the imperial forces—instead of seeking to destroy this rapidly spreading religious movement, it was far more effective to hijack it and baptize it in the wealth, power, and authority of the emperor. How easy it was for Constantine to seduce the leaders of the early church into official, state-sanctioned religious positions that came with authority, access, and great wealth.

Very soon, these bishops were answering not to God but to Constantine, who became the final say in Christian theology and practice and is largely responsible for establishing much of the beliefs and practices of Christians that continue to this day. The empire created Christianity by simply inserting Christian language and beliefs into the scaffolding of the pagan religions of the Roman world, and in doing so reduced Christianity to a religious practice rather than the radical sociopolitical movement that it was. In this move, Jesus was replaced as Lord with imperial power once again, which has remained the status quo of Christianity for the past 1,800 years or so. How many empires have declared themselves to be empowered by Christ? How often have Christian leaders cozied up to governments and tyrants, offering the blessing of God and the use of their faith to justify the actions of these leaders? Western history is littered with tragic examples.

Before this hijacking of the way of Jesus, the early Jesus followers organized themselves around the image of a sacrificial lamb. Jesus was a different kind of Lord whose power came from his willingness to lay down his life for the sake of love and justice, not from his divine authority or physical strength. Unlike the Roman emperors and hoped-for messiahs, Jesus' favor with God wasn't displayed through military might or from positions of authority—instead, the glory of God revealed in Jesus is seen in the vision of John in Revelation: "Then I saw a Lamb, looking as if it had been slain, standing at the center of the throne" (Rev. 5:6a NIV).

In God's ordering of the world, it is the gentle Lamb, slain for the sake of his own flock, that receives the authority and power. In God's ordering of the world, there is no use for chariots, swords, and wealth. Those work fine if one's goal is to perpetuate a worldly system of privilege, power, and violence. But if we are seeking to establish a world where shalom is the organizing principle, then we must be led by one whose power comes from a willingness to give up everything, even his very life, as a sacrificial offering.

A NEW KIND OF CHURCH

The lordship of Jesus was the principal belief and declaration for the earliest followers of Jesus. It was both theological—Jesus was God's Messiah—as well as political—Jesus was the rightful political ruler of the world. Both declarations required surrendering power and standing within the religious and social community, but also afforded the one who declared allegiance to Jesus' way a new kind of power. They were, in some sense, inducted into a not-so-secret society of people who were committed to making manifest the long-awaited reign of God right here and right now. This was done through the vehicle of the *ekklēsia*, which was not a religious institution at all, but referred to a regular political assembly that would happen in Roman colonies throughout the ancient empire. The Greek word translates roughly to "those who have been called out to conduct the business of the empire."

When Jesus used the word in Matthew 16:18, saying that Peter would be the "rock" upon which he would establish his church, he was surely parodying the structures of the empire as he often did, suggesting that his new movement would become an alternative government within the world yet called out from the world. Again, *ekklēsia* had *no* religious meaning at all in the Greco-Roman world and would have had no religious meaning when Jesus used it either. His disciples understood that he was describing a new ordering of the world that they were being invited to participate in that would one day rival and eventually overtake the Roman Empire. But this new movement, this new assembly, derived its power not from the emperor or the false gods and goddesses of the empire, but from the one true God of Abraham, Isaac, and Jacob. Its authority was derived from God and its mission was to transform "the kingdom of the world" into "the kingdom of our Lord and of his Messiah" (Rev. 11:15).

What then is the primary role of the "church"? The church established by Jesus is meant to be a community of citizens simultaneously of whatever empire they live in as well as the kingdom of God, who come together to demonstrate to themselves and the community around them God's ordering of the world. In this sense, the church is inherently political and is tremendously powerful. In another sense, this mission and posture strips the church of almost any true privilege it might hold in the eyes of an empire. The church is a vehicle of organized religion that utilizes religion as a means of community organizing.

The worship of the church, both in Jesus' day and in ours, has one primary ritual: the Eucharist, which was established by Jesus as a reminder of the method and the cost of belonging to his movement. To follow in this path of surrender and sacrifice, we are called to break open our lives and pour them out to create a more just and equal world. This is what Jesus did. And the cost is nothing less than our lives—both metaphorically and, for many, literally. Whenever one refuses allegiance to a political system but instead devotes oneself to a grassroots movement to reform society from the ground up, the powers that be will often respond with threats and violence.

Not only does the Eucharist symbolize these realities, but in and of itself, it was intended to be an act of justice. In the earliest days of the Jesus movement, the Eucharist wasn't merely a ritual where people are given a crumb of bread and a sip of wine—it was a full feast where all people, regardless of their ethnicity, gender, or social status, were welcome to come and feast freely. It would happen regularly—somewhere between daily and weekly—in many early Christian communities and was itself an alternative form of welfare. It provided a regular meal for anyone and everyone who desired to participate and was a taste of the world to come.[3]

The church that Jesus envisioned was much less a religious institution and much more a movement of grace and justice that didn't require people to convert to a new religion but instead asked people to commit to a way of seeing and being in the world. Rather than imitating the religious and political structures of power and privilege that existed in his world, he called his followers outside of such systems and into an informal network of communities that were dedicated to following his commands and transforming their neighborhoods through one subversive act of love at a time.

DISMANTLING CHRISTIAN HEGEMONY

Let's face it. It's easy to look at the texts of the New Testament and pontificate about how astray and corrupt the church has become—it's much harder to actually *do* anything about it. And while individual faith communities may be able to make significant transformation, the fact is that Christianity as an organized religion has become and remains one of the most powerful forces in the history of the world. But the power of the Christian religion is *not* the power that Jesus embodied. It is, in fact, the worldly, privileged, abusive power of empire.

When we come to this realization, there is only one faithful response: commit to exposing the hypocrisy of our religion and dismantling its structures of privilege piece by piece.

I know this sounds radical, and it is. But for those of us who find ourselves within the religious structures of Christianity and yet are awakening to just how disparate our religion has become from the message of Jesus, there is no other path. Jesus himself spoke of a day when the central institution of his religion—the temple—would be destroyed:

> Then, as some spoke of the temple, how it was adorned with beautiful stones and donations, He said, "These things which you see—the days will come in which not one stone shall be left upon another that shall not be thrown down." (Luke 21:5–6 NKJV)

Jesus was speaking both literally and metaphorically about what was to come of the temple. It's generally accepted that he was predicting the day that came in AD 70 when the temple was, in fact, destroyed by the Roman Empire. But in the context of his teachings, it's also safe to assume he was speaking of a day when the structures and powers that had co-opted the temple—both the empire and a class of religious leaders who exploited their own people—would be dismantled in exchange for something better. When speaking to the Samaritan women in John 4, Jesus phrases his prophecy quite differently:

> "Woman," Jesus replied, "believe me, a time is coming when you will worship the Father neither on this mountain nor in Jerusalem. You Samaritans worship what you do not know; we worship what we do know, for salvation is from the Jews. Yet a time

is coming and has now come when the true worshipers will worship the Father in the Spirit and in truth,
for they are the kind of worshipers the Father seeks.
God is spirit, and his worshipers must worship in the
Spirit and in truth." (John 4:21–24 NIV)

In the preceding verses, Jesus is conversing with this
woman about what mountain it is proper to worship God
on—a debate about which religious institution had divine
authority and actually represented the will of God. If Jesus
was interested in preserving the institution, he would have
clearly and simply argued that the temple in Jerusalem
was the correct temple and contained the very presence of
God. But he doesn't do that because he doesn't seem to
believe that. Instead he says, "A time is coming when you
will worship the Father neither on this mountain nor in
Jerusalem," reiterating the prophecy that the temple will
soon be destroyed. But instead of lamenting this reality,
he says, "True worshipers will worship the Father in the
Spirit and in truth, for they are the kind of worshipers the
Father seeks." In other words, the people who are *actually*
acceptable to God are not those who are participating in
the institution, but those outside of it, led by the Spirit and
committed to the truth.

This interpretation of Jesus' words is later confirmed
by the apostle Stephen as he is speaking to the Jewish San-
hedrin about the temple in Acts 7:48: "The Most High does
not live in houses made by human hands." Here is Stephen,
speaking to the highest authorities within the Jewish institution, declaring that God did not dwell in their temple,
which, if true, fundamentally undermined their authority
and claims of holiness. He's suggesting that, at very least,
Jesus reveals that no one ever needed an intermediary

between themselves and God, that the Spirit of God is a wild wind that blows wherever and to whomever it wishes. Openness to that Spirit and a hunger for truth is all that God seeks to commune with anyone.

If this was true then, how much truer is it today? Our institutions that have amassed billions of dollars, that have created never-ending hierarchies of "holiness" and power, that have spiritual and political control over billions of people around the world, all stand on the foundational claim that they represent and are ordained by God. Yet Jesus literally told us the opposite. The Most High doesn't live in temples, denominational offices, meetinghouses, or monasteries. More often than not, these institutions are the single biggest barriers standing in the way of people accessing the Divine. These institutions often reflect the power that comes from privilege, exploitation, and domination, not the power that is granted by God through self-sacrificial love for the good of another. That power cannot be contained or restrained. That power doesn't require a stamp of approval from a bishop. That power moves through the Spirit as it reveals Truth.

Which brings us back to the topic of Christian privilege and supremacy. Over the past two thousand years, the Christian religion has worked hard to take over the world by force. Despite the valiant narratives of missionaries sharing the gospel to desperate souls, the truth is that the reason Christianity has arrived at the position of privilege and power it currently enjoys is because it has slaughtered millions of people who stood in its way, enslaved and oppressed millions of people, and "converted" most of the others by force. Christianity, the religion, has been a tool of colonization by the empire, and in a very real sense has continued the oppressive legacy of the Roman Empire throughout the ages since the actual empire fell in AD 476.

This is one of the reasons why Christianity has endured—it has enjoyed the backing and support of imperial forces in just about every country that it has colonized. In every country where Christianity was granted political power, persecution of religious "minorities" (usually those who resisted conversion to Christianity) became the norm. Emperor Constantine's son Constantius II issued a decree in AD 341 that forbade pagan sacrifices—in countries where paganism had been the primary religion for thousands of years. Very quickly, it became a great benefit to be aligned with Christianity and a danger to the well-being of you and your family if you did not.

A MODERN "CHRISTIAN" NATION

Fast-forward to the age of the United States of America. While the nation was not *technically* founded as a Christian country, nearly all of the founders came from the British Empire, where Christianity was privileged and any other version of religion was eschewed. Christianity has enjoyed privilege from the very beginning of the nation's history— when the colonists arrived on the eastern shores and immediately began a genocide on the indigenous peoples of these lands, using Christian language and theology as their justification. In fact, early European colonizers received the official blessing of the pope to conquer and lay claim to "new lands" that did not belong to Christianity, which became part of a larger legal code known as the Doctrine of Discovery[4] that has been used up to the modern era as legal justification for the colonization of the North American continent.[5]

Can anyone truly look at the life and teachings of Jesus and also look at brazen imperial conquests done in his name to establish the modern American empire and not be profoundly disturbed? At the same time, can anyone be truly surprised that after more than 1,500 years of imperial Christianity as our inheritance, American Christianity has completely normalized and embraced holding the dominant and privileged position of power in this nation, whose stated values are to be a land where there are "no law(s) respecting an establishment of religion"?[6] And is it any wonder that in our era, we see a rise in violent white Christian nationalism at the very moment when white imperial Christianity is quickly losing adherents, influence, and authority over the political and societal institutions? White imperial Christianity is desperately grasping to maintain the power it has held for nearly two thousand years, with little hope of maintaining the undue privilege that it has had.

True followers of the renegade rabbi from Nazareth should rejoice at the loss of power and influence of the Christian religion. The religion of Christianity, in most of its forms, has nothing to do with Jesus. Instead of leading people to embrace the radical social, spiritual, and political teachings of Jesus, Christianity has simply made Jesus into the superior pagan god, an object of religious devotion and worship, but not someone who should be followed in any significant way. The people whose faith rises and falls on the inerrancy of the biblical story of Jesus' life, death, and resurrection have made the story of Jesus nothing more than a safe religious mythology that is reenacted every Sunday,

rather than the chronicles of a real man with a real vision
for restructuring our lives and our world to align with the
values of our Creator.

Today, our empires and institutions are being
drained of their unjust power. The time is coming, and
indeed is already here, when the *true* worshipers of God
will worship not in the halls of power, not in luxurious
megachurch campuses, but in the realm where the Spirit
is most present—among the least of these, the poor, the
religious minorities, the queer, the disabled, the sick, the
oppressed—and in the pursuit of the Truth that convicts us
and draws us collectively to our knees in sorrow for what
we have done in the name of Jesus, but the same Truth that
is a double-edged sword, setting free both the oppressed
and the oppressors.

The divine power that Jesus is granted in this hymn is
a power that comes from willingly kneeling in the dust and
dirt in order to lift others up. It's a power that comes from
his willingness to use every ounce of privilege and authority he had to help give the voiceless back their voice. Jesus
is exalted and declared to be the rightful Lord, not because
he conquered and converted the world, but because he
became a servant of all, the midwife of a more beautiful and
just world. Likewise, the same power will come to modern-
day Christians when we begin to tell the truth and allow the
Spirit to have its way among us. When we begin to confess
the sins of our religion that has *joyfully* destroyed cultures,
traditions, religions, and ways of life for countless tribes of
people around the globe. When we begin to admit that we
have used our religion to usurp power and exploit it for our
own benefit to the exclusion of the indigenous spiritual traditions in all the lands and peoples we've colonized. When
we finally confess that it has never been the Holy Spirit's

power at work within our institutions that have participated in and benefited from the xenophobic wars we've waged. When we finally admit that it has never been Jesus of Nazareth that we've worshiped, but Caesar, poorly disguised as Jesus.

The dismantling of the Christian hegemony is the true work and calling of every disciple of Jesus. We must fight to de-Christianize our countries, our cultures, our institutions, and our faith communities. We must begin to trust that the subversive and sacrificial way of Jesus is what can heal and transform the world into the "kingdom of God," and dispense with our addiction to worldly means of power. We must begin this work in our own individual lives and our own faith communities, as well as at the highest levels of religious hierarchy and government. Then and only then will the transformative, healing power of Jesus be unleashed in our lives, our communities, and our world.

PRACTICALLY HARNESSING OUR POWER

But how? This is admittedly a difficult question to answer. First, let's think through how we as individual disciples can begin to tap into this divine power that comes from living in the way of Jesus. Chances are that you live in a community where there are religious minorities. Regardless of whether you live in New York City or Jonesboro, Arkansas, there is probably a community of people who face marginalization because they do not ascribe to a Christian worldview. The truth is, most of us have never considered what daily challenges religious minorities (or other minorities) must face in cultures where we are the dominant people or where we hold power. One of the first challenges I encourage every reader to do is to research minority religious communities in your area, and then reach out and ask to meet with a member of that community simply so you can get to know them and their experience. The only agenda you should have for this meeting is to walk away with a better understanding of what it's like to be a member of their community in your community.

In this conversation, ask questions like these:

— Have you ever felt discriminated against or left out in our city because of your faith?
— What has your experience been practicing your faith in our community? Do you feel safe? Do you feel respected?
— How do you view Christians, based on your experience with us in this community?
— What are some of the barriers we've put up that keep you from feeling integrated into the life of our society?
— Do you feel as though your community has representation and access to leaders within our community?

These sorts of questions will give you the opportunity to hear uncomfortable truths about the ugly reality of privilege. It is important to remember that the entire purpose of these sorts of conversations is to gain empathic understanding and to form an actual relationship, not to use anyone for your own self-improvement. You shouldn't ask, "What can I/we do to be different?" or questions like that—that is your work to figure out through intentional reflection on what you learn and experience as you spend time hearing the stories and experience of your minority neighbor. But it is also essential that you *do* take time to contemplate what you have learned and think of ways that you individually or you within your community can help to dismantle the barriers and biases that keep minorities—religious, ethnic, sexual and gender, disabled, and so on—from being fully included and equal within your community. This is a time for you to use the power granted by your privilege to elevate others' voices and to make substantial changes wherever possible.[7]

Next, let's think through what a local faith community can do to utilize this strange power. When I was serving as the pastor of a church, I wrestled with this question daily. On one hand, I deeply appreciated the rituals and religious functions of Christianity and loved "performing" them within the context of a worship service. But as I became more convinced that this function was, first, not what Jesus ever intended, and second, increasingly irrelevant to our culture, I wondered how we might rethink what our church looked like and how we channeled our time and resources.

My very first realization was that most churches spend most of their money on maintaining an organization and building rather than doing actual work that transforms their neighborhoods. As I sat with my small church's nearly half-million-dollar yearly budget and realized that a good third of the funds we raised went to the mortgage, building maintenance, and salaries, I felt my stomach turn in knots. Every day I would walk up to our campus and find a new person experiencing homelessness sleeping on our porch. Every day I thought about what it would take to get that person some food, some clothes, and a cheap apartment. I realized that for the amount we were paying every month in mortgage, we could easily provide for a good portion of the individuals who found their way to our campus.

Then I looked at what we were paying folks, including myself—very little, to be honest. While I loved the fact that I was able to be paid to do ministry full-time, the fact is, the hundred thousand dollars or so that we spent on a few salaries could have gone a long way to start many initiatives in our community to help dismantle white supremacy, fight climate change, and provide for those in need. And the meager sum left over after general operating expenses—usually not more than maybe a few hundred dollars—did very little to help anyone or anything in our church or beyond.

I also struggled to figure out how we could justify gathering a couple hundred folks every Sunday morning for a glorified social gathering and TED talk where we banged on and on about justice and God's vision for the world, but then sent the congregation home without provoking them to take any substantial action collectively or individually to make Jesus' social vision a reality in their lives or sphere of influence.

Any pastors (or congregants, for that matter) who seriously wrestle with the social and political ramifications of Jesus' authentic message will find themselves in this perplexing space. Religion isn't what Jesus came to create, yet religion is the primary means through which people learn about and commit to follow Jesus in our world today. Jesus was arguably anti-institution, and yet today his name is the central focus of countless millions of institutions. Some even could argue that Jesus was not interested in being an object of worship, but rather a teacher who was followed, and yet billions of people gather every Sunday to sing praises to his name. What are we to do when this has become our reality?

I never was able to find a single clear answer for what our church *should* do or what I should do as a Christian. I also don't believe there is a single answer that fits all people or faith communities. On the surface, the most obvious answer seemed to be to sell our buildings, fire our staff, cancel our worship services, and use our resources for social good. And I actually *did* do some of that—after years of work, we were able to sell our campus with the intention to reinvest in another property (mortgage free) that would be more multifunctional to support outreach and justice initiatives. That felt like a small step in the correct direction for our community—but still fell vastly short of the profound call of Jesus.

Thankfully, Jesus begins his gospel proclamation with a call to believe and repent—meaning that following his path requires believing in that which is not evident and continually expanding our perspectives and changing our direction. We shouldn't expect to break out of the systems of our culture and religion and begin walking a radically subversive path overnight. The fact is that religion is a profoundly helpful and necessary part of human society—and a religion focused on Jesus has helped and can help us live a better, more purposeful life. But what I am saying is that for anyone who is committed to the kenotic way of Jesus, things cannot stay there.

If our faith is only about spiritual fulfillment and community, then we are a part of the problem, not the solution. Our job is to, day by day, gradually conform our lives and our churches to the way of Jesus, asking how we can leverage our resources, our privilege, and our power each day for the good of those on the margins. In the church, these conversations should take place at every level, from small groups of laypeople to the board and staff. What would it look like if church members began hosting a Eucharist meal every week in the church and invited absolutely everyone to come and gather for a free meal—no strings attached? What would it look like if the church committed to cut spending and increase giving to ensure that 50 percent of the monthly income was going out the door and into the community? What if the church worked to ensure that its campus was being used seven days a week by freely offering it to justice groups, activists, artists, and entrepreneurs to organize, educate, and create?

Doing these things is not intended to increase our sense of faithfulness—they only scratch the surface of what's truly required of us. But such sacrificial actions enable us to tap into a new kind of power—we are not reliant on government or politicians or agencies to create the change we know is needed in our world. Instead, we become the change agents. This doesn't mean that we shouldn't engage politically—we very much should. But our power is in utilizing our resources and our privilege for others, which is something that political leaders can only *aspire* to do. We cannot wait for the world to change. We should not wait for the political process to unfold. If we are truly to harness the power that comes from the proclamation "Jesus Christ is Lord," then we must be willing to take into our own hands the ultimate responsibility of renewing our world by working alongside God to heal and redeem the world.

If the Kenosis Hymn makes anything clear, it's that traditional power schemes and politics as usual have little hope of fixing things. They have the priorities flipped. They're about grasping for power, storing up privilege, and serving the interests of a few. The divine power manifest in following Jesus' path can do far more than set the world to right—which is no small thing. It can transform the human heart through the unfailing power of love.

DISCUSSION QUESTIONS

1. What would it look like for the first to become last and the last to become first in your community? What role might you play in this reversal?

2. What does it mean that phrases like "＿＿ is Lord," "receive the sacrament," and even "*ekklēsia*" had powerful meanings in the secular Roman world before Jesus gave those terms new meaning for his kingdom?

3. What would it mean to practice a "pre-Constantinian" Christianity? What is the problem with Christianity being aligned with empires and governments?

4. The author says, "The church that Jesus envisioned was much less a religious institution and much more a movement of grace and justice that didn't require people to convert to a new religion but instead asked people to commit to a way of seeing and being in the world." How might the church today become less of an institution and more of the movement Jesus envisioned?

5. How do you personally walk in the tension between institutionalized religion and following in the way of Jesus? Have you ever felt the discomfort with the church's use of money that the author describes?

6. What are some ways you have seen the white Christian hegemony embodied in your daily life? Who are those most negatively impacted by it in your community?

Chapter 8

FEAR AND TREMBLING

Therefore, my dear friends, as you have always obeyed—not only in my presence, but now much more in my absence—continue to work out your salvation with fear and trembling, for it is God who works in you to will and to act in order to fulfill his good purpose.

—Philippians 2:12–13 NIV

Fear is the opposite of love. This is probably the single most important grounding principle of my own Christian faith and theology. This became so important to me when I was experiencing the full force of evangelical patriarchy as a student at Moody Bible Institute. I was struggling to reconcile my queer sexuality with my white evangelical Christian faith and was forced to have dozens of meetings with professors and administrators from the school who continually used fear as a means of controlling me. There was fear of being expelled for not aligning with Moody's beliefs, fear of being disqualified from ministry as a pastor, and ultimately, fear that God would condemn my soul to eternal torment if I embraced a "homosexual lifestyle." The truth is that if you seek to control people, fear is the most effective tactic . . . until they realize that the thing they're being threatened with doesn't exist. That's when liberation emerges.

As I lay in my bed having a panic attack after one particularly painful meeting with the dean, I did what I was taught to do as a good evangelical boy—I picked up my Bible and began to seek wisdom from God. It was in this moment that I found myself reading these liberating words:

> God is love. Whoever lives in love lives in God, and God in them. This is how love is made complete among us so that we will have confidence on the day of judgment: In this world we are like Jesus. There is no fear in love. But perfect love drives out fear, because fear has to do with punishment. The one who fears is not made perfect in love. (1 John 4:16b–18 NIV)

I was being taught to fear God. To live each day afraid of God's judgment upon me if I ever slipped up and stepped off the straight and narrow path. But in a moment, this verse shone a spotlight on the vengeful, judgmental god of my evangelical faith and revealed that he didn't exist. God *is* love. That is God's identity and nature—they are synonymous. And Love casts out *fear of punishment*. Therefore, anyone who uses the "judgment of God" as a tactic to force us into conformity with their agenda is proving that they are not of God and do not know the God revealed in Jesus. After all, *there is no fear in love.* And just like that, the mythic god that was being used to abuse and suppress me died in my mind, and I committed to rejecting *any* theology that used fear as a central tenet. Instead, I committed to living a spiritual path in which "love is made complete among us," which the writer simply and succinctly summarizes as being "in this world . . . like Jesus." Rejecting fear, embracing love, being like Jesus. That is the best summary of my Christian faith, and it truly did save my life.

This message is truly liberating, not just for those of us with spiritual trauma, but for every person that has ever been oppressed. Oppression is fueled by fear. Whenever we can demonize and provoke terror in the hearts of people, they can be manipulated and controlled in the most malevolent ways.[1] But when people can see past the lies and deception and choose the path of believing in their own belovedness (and therefore dignity and equity) as well as understand that Love is the ground of all being, then they can find strength and power to overcome and overturn any and every oppressive system and structure.

THE ONE REASON TO FEAR

However, despite all of this, there *is* a singular productive role for *fear,* and it is discussed in Paul's concluding instruction following the Kenosis Hymn in Philippians 2: "continue to work out your salvation with fear and trembling." Now, if we are using the inherited theology of Christianity the religion, we may interpret that verse as an admonition to be fearful for our salvation—meaning being saved from hell when we die. Even though this is how this verse is often preached in many pulpits, that interpretation divorces it completely from the context of the Kenosis Hymn that precedes it. This isn't about going to heaven or being saved from hell at all—the salvation being referenced here is *Jesus'* version of salvation, not Paul's. It's about personal and social transformation through *living kenotically,* obeying the teachings and conforming to the example of Jesus.

Salvation is about *wholeness* and *restoration.* In fact, the Greek word used here is *sōtēria,* a term drawn from the Greek myth of the goddess Soteria, who was called upon to deliver people out of harm's way. The idea behind salvation is that impending destruction is imminent—not because God is judging us, but because we have built our lives and world on a foundation of sand. The oppressive ways in which we have come to operate in the world *always* end up bringing destruction. The ways of empire have *never* succeeded—every empire ultimately falls due to its own greed and intoxication with its self-prescribed privilege. The warning given in the Gospels by Jesus and repeated here by Paul is that *if* we don't work hard to start living in the kenotic path, which subverts the dominant operating systems of our world and works to level the playing fields, establish justice, and perpetuate wholeness for everyone, *then* we have very good reason to be afraid—our individual and collective destruction is assured.

This perhaps has never been clearer than in the modern era—human greed, xenophobia, and suppression of truth have brought us to the brink of global destruction. This is not an overstatement in the least—scientists tell us that if we do not change the trajectory of climate change in the next six years, the effects on our environment will be irreversible and will likely lead to mass extinction of our species and destruction of much of the world.[2] Even *this* has its roots in privilege—human privilege, a belief that human beings are superior to all other created species and entitled to use the natural world for our own ends—and has been primarily caused by the humans with the most privilege while most negatively impacting those with the least. Our exploitation of creation for our own benefit has literally brought us to the brink of death—and frankly, it seems that humans are burying our heads in the sand and choosing to believe that such destruction could never actually happen to us, which is a stunning example of just how blind privilege and entitlement can make us. If there was ever a moment for legitimate fear and trembling, it is now.

Destruction is the result of any long-term exploitation of one's privilege—greed and selfishness always backfire in the end. White privilege has created systems and structures that are unable to stand as justice and equity roll forth like a river in our society—and this will create a sense of loss for millions of white people. The pain and fears of, for instance, the white working-class family in the midwestern United States are very real. In different eras of history, when white supremacy was even more dominant, it was far easier for white working-class families to succeed at the expense of the exploitation and exclusion of people of color. The system of whiteness was built upon the expectation that such oppression would continue in perpetuity. But justice and truth are slowly prevailing, and as they do, the system of whiteness is facing collapse, and with it the inherited expectation of success, comfort, and prosperity for white working-class Americans.

The pain the privileged feel when equity begins to be realized is real. There is often a cost. It will, in fact, become more difficult and take more work for white people to succeed when the system of white privilege is dismantled. But that is not oppression—it's *fairness.* It respects no identity as better than others, offers no advantages, and offers everyone an equal opportunity to run the race of "success," with winning being wholly dependent on talent, effort, and persistence alone. While many white people have bought into the illusion that it was only through hard work and stamina that our ancestors "succeeded," when our eyes are opened to the reality of privilege, we begin to see that the race our ancestors ran was rigged in our favor and against people of color, and actually was fueled by their exploitation for our own "success." As we begin to realize and reckon with these realities, we also need to realize that as the systems of whiteness are dismantled, there will be an era of great discomfort and a sense of loss for many of us. But this is the consequence of the unjust systems that our ancestors created, and if we are to truly see the justice of God established on earth, we are required to pass through this moment of fear and trembling.

But privileged people shouldn't fear things getting more "difficult" for us, but rather, we should fear the results of what will happen if things do not. Greed and exploitation *always* result in mutually assured destruction, both of those who exploit and those who are being exploited. As the mountains are lowered and valleys are exalted, we must rejoice, for only through this subversive reckoning can the more beautiful world our hearts know is possible become a reality. This is indeed God's judgment upon us, but it is not retributive, it is restorative. When we begin to function as a collective, caring and sacrificing for the good of one another in all our diversity, all of us will flourish. Through losing our position of privilege, all of us together will gain immensely. It is counterintuitive and it certainly won't feel like gain initially, but if we truly trust in the social-spiritual vision of Jesus, we should have confidence that in a world of equality, abundance will flow freely for us all.

WE'RE THE HOPE WE'VE BEEN LOOKING FOR

A just and equal world is indeed God's will and purpose for us, as Paul writes in Philippians 2:13. This is where the entire trajectory of the Bible is pointing, toward the restoration of the world to its Edenic state, a flourishing garden of interconnectivity and mutuality among all created things. This is what is referenced by the word "heaven" throughout the Scriptures: not some magical land in the sky, but rather a renewed and redeemed earth. The Jewish hope was always that God would restore the world and establish a government of justice for all. The prophet Isaiah describes the hope of the messianic age in these profound words:

> The wolf will live with the lamb,
> the leopard will lie down with the goat,
> the calf and the lion and the yearling together;
> and a little child will lead them.
> The cow will feed with the bear,
> their young will lie down together,
> and the lion will eat straw like the ox.
> The infant will play near the cobra's den,
> and the young child will put its hand into the
>   viper's nest.
> They will neither harm nor destroy
> on all my holy mountain,
> for the earth will be filled with the knowledge
>   of the LORD
> as the waters cover the sea.
>   *(Isa. 11:6–9 NIV)*

Notice the contrasts Isaiah is seeking to make: in nearly every example, he is describing God's ideal world as one where opposites live peacefully and cooperatively with one another. There is no competition, no exploitation, no manipulation. Wolves and lambs live together without one fearing the other. The same for leopards and goats, calves and lions, and children in the midst of all of these wild animals. This vision is one where every realm of creation is living in harmony and interconnectivity.

Notice what Paul seems to suggest in Philippians 2:13: the means of establishing the world of harmony in this eschatological vision is God working *in us*. This is very different from the hope proclaimed in many churches today, that in the end times God will come and personally set the world straight by force. Instead, the messianic plan of Jesus and the teaching of Paul is that God desires to work in and through human beings to create the kind of world where the kenotic way of Jesus is the normative way of existing and interacting. Instead of promising that if we wait long enough or if we pray hard enough, we can call heaven down to earth, this teaches that we must take the initiative to make this a reality. Which is, again, a reason for some fear and trembling.

God seems to believe in humanity far more than most of us humans do. There are moments of transcendent compassion, where we see glimmers of the potential of humanity to do the right thing and act selflessly for the good of others, but those seem quite rare, don't they? We can think of saints and heroes whose hagiographies often exaggerate their otherworldly sense of compassion, covering their flaws and shortcomings from public view, but is this small community of extraordinary humans enough to save the planet from destruction? Jesus and Paul suggest that it is not.

This is where faith comes in. The Christian hope is and has always been that God, working through ordinary humans, will indeed redeem and renew our world. This is what the incarnation and kenosis together demonstrate. Jesus is an icon, an example of who we are to be—regular human beings who do the work to connect with God and become conduits of divine love, who then go into the world allowing that love to flow through us to the broken places of creation. For whatever reason, our Creator has not chosen to simply come down and fix our mess, but has chosen to allow us to walk through struggle and the consequences of our greed, sending reminders that if only we open ourselves up to God's will instead of our own, healing and salvation can come at last.

This doesn't seem likely, if I'm honest. Our track record of perpetual waywardness as humans seems to suggest that we're doomed. But then I think to the perennial story of the Jewish people, which is the story of us all; the journey to the promised land is filled with continuous struggles and challenges, many of their own making. Time and time again, the Hebrew people lose their way, doubt the goodness of God, and fall into idolatry. The path to arrive at the land of redemption is anything but straight and narrow. But remember, in the midst of it all, God continues to show up to guide them as a pillar of fire at night and a pillar of cloud by day. Time and time again, God sends prophets and messengers to remind them of the way they should go. And eventually, by God's grace, they do at last arrive at the promised land.

I believe the same will be true for humanity, collectively. As Teilhard de Chardin wrote, "The future is more beautiful than all the pasts."[3] We've been through the refining fires, and frankly, we've been through the infernos of hell. We will likely face those flames again in the future. We will likely face more self-inflicted destruction. Yet through it all, we're reminded that "it is God who works in you to will and to act in order to fulfill his good purpose." There is now and has always been a remnant of people who are dedicated to the will of God, who carry forth God's good purposes for the world. And the more who awaken to God's will, the more whose lives are transformed by the self-giving love of Christ, the more who are enraptured by Jesus' vision for what the world can become, the nearer we will progress toward that beautiful future where the lion and the lamb dwell together.

But as poetic as that far-off day may be, the truth is that the work to be done, the actions required of us by our Creator, are radical and drastic. While individual acts of charity are tremendous starts to move us forward, truly revolutionary actions will be required of us if we are to see that day. The world as we've constructed it is not, nor has it ever been, sustainable. The systems of greed and dominance that operate in nearly every country around the world will need to be abandoned completely, allowing a new, collectivistic mode of being to emerge in its place. Our economies must be reformed completely, functioning out of the truth that there is more than enough for everyone of everything that we truly need if we are willing to suspend our impulse toward avarice. The ways that we relate to the planet must change immediately, understanding that we are not gods over the natural world, but intimate partners with it.

A REVOLUTION OF FAITH OVER FEAR

Nothing less than a revolution is required of us. A revolution of self-giving love. A revolution that consistently asks us to reassess our privilege and power, leveraging it for the good of others. A revolution of consciousness, where we work to remove our tribal lenses of competition and instead begin to acknowledge that there is no separation between us and anything—for in God "we live and move and have our being" (Acts 17:28). But all of these revolutions begin with a revolution of faith—the belief in human potential, infused with divinity, to live the kenotic life and to re-create our systems and structures after the kenotic power of God. Again, this is understandably hard for us to believe in the modern world, as the fate of the earth literally hangs in the balance.

But faith overcomes fear. Kenotic love casts fear far from us. Fear must not be what compels us to action. When fear takes over, our higher levels of thinking are suppressed and we revert to our most tribal, reptilian impulses. This is no time for moving backward. This is a time for us to do the hard work, to refuse to be reactionary, to trust in the wisdom of God revealed through Jesus, and to transcend our former assumptions about the world and our relationship to it. With the ethical, scientific, technological, and theological advances of our world, we have never had a better chance at bringing our collective energies together and changing the ordering of our world in a generative, rather than destructive, way. And so we have good reason for faith. We have good reason to believe that we can overcome, with God's help.

But sacrifice is required, no, demanded of each and every one of us. We must be willing to take a leap into the unknown, trusting that *if* we really do give up our power and privilege for the good of others, if we do begin living a life of selflessness instead of greed, if we do begin to acknowledge and make reparations for the systems set up to benefit some at the exclusion of others, that God's Spirit will work through those sacrifices to birth a new world that our minds can scarcely even begin to conceive of. This is a time of risk and innovation. This is a time for bold leaps and not baby steps. This is a time when we are invited to throw caution to the wind, because there are but two choices ahead of us—renewal or destruction. We've literally got nothing left to lose.

In a moment like this, the prophetic words written in Deuteronomy 30:19–20 resonate:

This day I call the heavens and the earth as witnesses
against you that I have set before you life and death,
blessings and curses. Now choose life, so that you
and your children may live and that you may love
the LORD your God, listen to his voice, and hold fast
to him. For the LORD is your life, and he will give
you many years in the land he swore to give to your
fathers, Abraham, Isaac and Jacob. (NIV)

This is a moment of reckoning, and our choices are clear.
This choice conjures up fear and trembling within us, as it
should. We, like the people of Israel long ago, must choose
whether we and our children will *live*—period. And how
do we make that choice? We must "listen to [God's] voice"
because "[God] is your life." If we "hold fast" to God's
will and way, revealed in the kenotic outpouring of love by
Jesus, God will give us "many years in the land," or rather,
"on the land." While we may be more acutely aware of how
significant this choice is for us in this moment of history,
the truth is this same choice has always been facing humanity. When we cut ourselves off from that still, small voice of
God within us that convicts us when we choose greed and
exploitation over equity and justice, when we choose the
way of death, perpetuating cycles of retribution and degra-
dation of life, we are choosing destruction for all.

But even now, as the clock of human destiny is but
one minute from midnight, God extends to us a choice
and an imperative: *choose the path that leads to flourishing.*
Choose to confront systemic racism. Choose to confront
xenophobia. Choose to confront sexism, classism, nationalism, and Christian supremacy. Choose the better way
that our hearts have always known was right, but that we've
been conditioned to suppress. If we will, today, commit

to repentance and realigning with the will of God in the kenotic way of Jesus, I do believe, with every fiber of my being, that our salvation will draw nigh.

DISCUSSION QUESTIONS

1. Do you believe that there is a role for fear in faith? What are some beliefs that people hold that may cause them to be afraid? What would it mean for love to cast out fear in those cases?
2. Does "salvation," to you, primarily mean eternal life after death, or something else? Is it hard for you to define salvation in terms of earthly restoration and wholeness?
3. Do you think that most people experience "fear and trembling" over how close our greed and corruption have brought us to destruction?
4. Do you agree with the author that "God seems to believe in humanity far more than most of us humans do"? How might God use humans to redeem and renew the world?
5. Do you fear losing your privilege? What might it cost you for the playing field to be leveled?
6. What would it look like to choose faith over fear? What tangible actions are you willing to take in order to align yourself with the will of God and "choose life"?

Conclusion

FROM INSURRECTION
TO RESURRECTION

On Wednesday, January 6, 2021, I sat in my bedroom just
ten blocks from the US Capitol. Just days before, I had
moved across the country from San Diego to Washington,
DC, to begin a new season of my ministry doing full-time
advocacy work. The day before, I had gone out to pick up
lunch and noticed that the city had been filled with military vehicles and increased police presence in anticipation
of a rally and protests being held by supporters of President Donald Trump the next day. In my short walk, I had
come across dozens of tourists shuffling off the Metro trains
with their luggage, adorned with red "Make America Great
Again" hats and exhibiting a rowdy energy. I hurried home
with my lunch and prepared for what was certain to be a
wild day in the nation's capital. But I didn't know just how
out of hand it would become.

On Wednesday morning, I greeted my roommate,
who works in the Capitol, where our legislators would be
meeting to certify the electoral college victory of President-
elect Joe Biden. "Be safe out there today!" I said. "I'll try,"
he replied, with a nervous laugh. Within a few hours, I
began to hear a cacophony of sirens and helicopters around
my house, and I turned on the news to see thousands of
people storming the Capitol, breaking windows, beating
police, and successfully halting the certification of the votes

as lawmakers were evacuated from the building. Earlier that morning, President Trump had provoked this crowd with emphatic declarations that the election had been stolen, that he had won in a landslide, but that socialist forces deep within the government were working to ensure he didn't remain in office because he was fighting on behalf of the "American people" (by which, of course, he meant white, straight, cisgender, Christian Americans).

Now, I will not try to offer a comprehensive analysis of how America got to this dark moment—it would certainly take more than a book this size to even broach the subject. But what I will say is this: This moment of insurrection—incited by a president whose primary message was rooted in preserving systemic privilege for white, straight, able-bodied, Christian US citizens, and returning the nation to an era when every politician was a "Christian," when people of color were not a "threat" to white people's jobs because they wouldn't be hired anyway, when women were treated as second-class citizens, when LGBTQ+ relationships were criminalized, and when the only acceptable immigrants were those coming from Europe—was one of the most blatant reminders of just how powerful, prevalent, and destructive privilege is.

In an era of history when America, along with many other nations, is really beginning to grapple with the dark beliefs, laws, and practices that form the very foundation of the nation, and is beginning to slowly and imperfectly work to dismantle systemic injustices, those who have been blinded by their privilege and power are feeling deeply threatened and afraid, and they have shown that they will use every ounce of privilege and power they have left to fight—with literal violence—to preserve the status quo. As we've explored at length in this book, when the mountains are lowered and the valleys exalted, it's easy for those on the mountaintops to feel that what they are experiencing is unfair and unjust. If you've lived with undeserved advantage for generations, when the moment of reckoning comes when you are asked to forfeit that privilege for the sake of equity, such a request can feel like too much to ask.

Which is why, in a moment like this, it is essential that all of us who claim to follow the way of Jesus should pause and reflect on how we will respond to this moment of our collective history: Will we be a people of insurrection or resurrection? Will we be a people set against the movement of subversive justice that Jesus called for or will we be a people who yearn for the renewal of all things, in which all people are at last seen as the children of God, worthy of equal dignity and opportunity?

If our version of Christianity fuels us to fight to preserve our privilege, to keep the structures of empire in place to benefit people who believe like us, look like us, and love like us, then perhaps we should take some time to reflect on the kenotic example of Jesus and ask whether we're truly interested in following his path. Jesus was never acting for his own benefit. He understood that when each of us acts selflessly for the good of others, then everyone will be taken care of, everyone will have opportunity, and everyone will ultimately be led toward a life of flourishing.

It is true that Jesus himself launched an insurrection of sorts against the systems of privilege and dominance in his world, but his insurrection sought to overturn the empire not by force, but rather through subversive acts of love. Therefore the better and ancient word for Jesus' actions is *resurrection*—raising up that Edenic vision of how the world was created to be from the ashes of the endless destruction and greed of many human systems of governance. The resurrection that Jesus promises is not one of personal benefit or personal reward, but a collective one. Jesus calls this the "renewal of all things" (Matt. 19:28), where every aspect of creation is included in this restoration of justice and righteousness to our world.

But this resurrection cannot happen on its own. This resurrection is contingent upon human beings, you and me, choosing to take up our crosses and follow in the footsteps of our renegade rabbi. It requires us to return, again and again, to the "mind of Christ" that Paul describes with the Kenosis Hymn, where we willingly, recklessly give up our privilege and power to bring healing and restoration to those who are broken, cast down, and oppressed. It requires us to orient ourselves every day toward the cross, where Jesus was executed by empire to show us where the road of empire leads—always to death and destruction. We must reclaim the cross as an icon of the way we are to live— subversively working to undo the systems that perpetuate prejudice and bias, willing to sacrifice our own advantages so that others can have a fair shake at life.

Christianity today has become one of the most powerful tools to promote and protect racism, sexism, homophobia, transphobia, Christian supremacy, and so much more. Christianity bears almost no resemblance to the Christ it claims to worship. If our world is to begin to experience the resurrection that we long for, it must begin with followers of Jesus being willing to abandon "Christianity" for the sake of following Jesus. If your faith is more concerned with doctrines, dogmas, and upholding traditions than with daily seeking to use your time, energy, and money to undo the damage that your own privilege has wrought, then can you truly claim to be following Jesus?

This question isn't posed in judgment. It's a question that I really believe the church must consider. Is the heartbeat of our faith religious devotion, theological ruminations, and liturgical traditions? None of these things are bad, but if they are the extent of our faith, then we ought to be honest that we are actually *cultural Christians* rather than authentic disciples of Jesus. In fact, being a disciple of Jesus doesn't even require church membership or confessing creeds; one simply needs to believe in the vision that Jesus cast for a more just and equal world, and begin applying his teachings to our lives in an attempt to work in his spirit to make it a reality. Jesus himself made this clear, saying:

> Not everyone who says to me, "Lord, Lord," will enter the kingdom of heaven, but only the one who does the will of my Father who is in heaven. (Matt. 7:21)

Many are happy to sing songs of praise to Jesus, many desire the benefits of claiming to be a Christian in our society, but very few seem to be ready to *do the will of God,* which is prerequisite to entering the kingdom that Jesus envisioned. This passage isn't primarily about salvation beyond the grave, but rather about those who will enter the more just world here and now because they have chosen to actively live in the pattern of self-emptying that Jesus embodied. If you want to experience resurrection, you have to live it. If you want to overcome the forces of insurrection, you must live in the pattern of resurrection, which requires dying to the pursuit of privilege and power and giving birth to a new way of living in the world.

This is a moment of reckoning. Whoever you are, wherever you may be in the world, whatever your political or theological bent, you are being asked to choose. Will we follow the path of empire, the path of privilege, the path of exploitation, or will we follow the path that calls us to come and die to give birth to a new kind of living, a new kind of being, not just for us, but for all of creation? This is not a choice any of us can make lightly, but the consequences of this choice have rarely stood out so clearly as they do in our era. The planet is crying out, oppressed peoples are raising their voices, and the privileged and powerful are raging. The time has come for followers of Jesus to begin following in bold, prophetic, and costly ways. It is my sincere hope and prayer that each of us will awaken to the Spirit's call and respond with brave and faithful commitment to living in the way of Jesus.

May it be.

NOTES

CHAPTER 1: THE PROBLEM OF PRIVILEGE

1. *Merriam-Webster's Collegiate Dictionary,* 11th ed. (2003), s.v. "privilege."

2. Justin D. García, "Privilege (Social Inequality)," in *Salem Press Encyclopedia* (2018).

3. Scott Jaschik, "Black Activists Need Not Apply," *Inside Higher Ed,* September 10, 2018, www.insidehighered.com/admissions/article/2018/09/10/study-suggests-admissions-officers-are-more-responsive-Black.

4. Cheryl Staats et al., *State of the Science: Implicit Bias Review,* 2017 ed. (Columbus, OH: Kirwan Institute for the Study of Race and Ethnicity, Ohio State University, 2017), 10, http://kirwaninstitute.osu.edu/implicit-bias-training/resources/2017-implicit-bias-review.pdf.

5. See Ibram X. Kendi, *How to Be an Antiracist* (New York: One World, 2019).

CHAPTER 2: PARADOXOLOGY

1. Richard A. Horsley, *Jesus and Empire: The Kingdom of God and the New World Disorder* (Minneapolis: Fortress Press, 2006), 184.

2. Obery M. Hendricks Jr., *The Politics of Jesus: Rediscovering the True Revolutionary Nature of the Teachings of Jesus and How They Have Been Corrupted* (New York: Doubleday, 2006), 184.

3. For the entire speech, see "Obama's 2006 Speech on Faith and Politics," *New York Times,* June 28, 2006, https://www.nytimes.com/2006/06/28/us/politics/2006obamaspeech.html.

4. Quoted in Martin Yee, "Tullian Tchividjian on the Sermon on the Mount—The Glorious Impossibilty," blog post, Lutheran Theology Study Group of Singapore, October 27, 2012, lutherantheologystudygroup.blogspot.com/2012/10/tullian-tchividjian-on-sermon-on-mount.html.

5. A great book that digs into the divisions between the early disciples and Paul is James Tabor, *Paul and Jesus: How the Apostle Transformed Christianity* (New York: Simon and Schuster, 2021).

6. Walter Hansen, *The Letter to the Philippians* (Grand Rapids: Wm. B. Eerdmans, 2009), 15.

7. See Kelsi Watters, "Solidarity and Suffering: Liberation Christology from Black and Womanist Perspectives," in *Obsculta* 12, no. 1 (2019): 78–107, https://digitalcommons.csbsju.edu/obsculta/vol12/iss1/8; and Karen Bautista Enriquez, "Interrupting the Conversation on Kenosis and Sunyata: Buddhist and Christian Women in Search of the Relational Self" (PhD thesis, Boston College, 2011).

8. Thanks to Jodi Belcher for her essay, "Subversion through Subjection: A Feminist Reconsideration of Kenosis in Christology and Christian Discipleship" (Master's thesis, Vanderbilt University, 2008), which helped me to articulate this perspective; https://ir.vanderbilt.edu/bitstream/handle/1803/11686/thesis_final_jlabelcher.pdf.

9. Sarah Coakley, *Powers and Submissions: Spirituality, Philosophy, and Gender* (Malden, MA: Blackwell, 2002), 37.

10. Coakley, *Powers and Submissions*, 36.

CHAPTER 3: A NEW MINDSET

1. If you don't know, *Lizzie McGuire* was the best show on Disney Channel in the early 2000s. It was about a girl and her struggles with middle and high school. Lizzie was played by the incomparable Hilary Duff.

2. Heinz Kreissig, *Die sozialen Zusammenhänge des Judäischen Krieges: Klassen und Klassenkampf im Palästina des 1. Jahrhunderts v. u. Z.* (Berlin: Akademie Verlag, 1970), 17–87.

3. Joseph Chaim Wertheimer and Eliezer Halevi Grunhut, *Midrash Shir Hashirim: Printed from a Geniza Manuscript* (Jerusalem: Ktav Yad Vasefer Institute, 1971), Rabba 2:12.

4. Catholic Campaign for Human Development, "The Population of Poverty USA," citing statistics from the US Department of Agriculture, https://www.povertyusa.org/facts; US Census Bureau, "Quick Facts," https://www.census.gov/quickfacts/fact/map/US/HSD410219.

CHAPTER 4: OWNING OUR IDENTITY

1. MyUSF, "Check Your Privilege," University of San Francisco, n.d., https://myusf.usfca.edu/student-life/intercultural-center/check-your-privilege.

2. US Census Bureau, "Nearly 1 in 5 People Have a Disability in the U.S., Census Bureau Reports," July 25, 2012, https://www.census.gov/newsroom/releases/archives/miscellaneous/cb12-134.html.

3. "What Is the Integral Approach?" Integral Life, March 15, 2021, integrallife.com/what-is-integral-approach/.

4. To see Robert Keegan's work in this area, read *The Evolving Self: Problem and Process in Human Development* (Cambridge, MA: Harvard University Press, 1982), and for

James W. Fowler's work, read *Stages of Faith: The Psychology of Human Development and the Quest for Meaning* (New York: HarperCollins, 1995).

CHAPTER 5: EXCHANGING ROLES

1. See Richard Rohr and Andreas Ebert, *The Enneagram: A Christian Perspective* (New York: Crossroad, 2001).

CHAPTER 6: OBEDIENCE UNTO DEATH

1. For a deeper exploration of the revolutionary political message of Jesus, see Obrey M. Hendricks, Jr., *The Politics of Jesus: Rediscovering the True Revolutionary Nature of Jesus' Teachings and How They Have Been Corrupted* (New York: Doubleday, 2006).

2. Cynthia Bourgeault, *The Wisdom Jesus: Transforming Heart and Mind—A New Perspective on Christ and His Message* (Boston: New Seeds Books, 2008), 63–64.

3. Richard Rohr and Andreas Ebert, *The Enneagram: A Christian Perspective* (New York: Crossroad, 2001), 81–82.

4. See Richard Rohr, *Falling Upward: A Spirituality for the Two Halves of Life* (San Francisco: Jossey-Bass, 2011).

5. Brené Brown, "The Midlife Unraveling," *Brené Brown* (blog), May 24, 2018, brenebrown.com/blog/2018/05/24/the -midlife-unraveling/.

6. Bourgeault, *The Wisdom Jesus*, 67.

7. Mevlana Jalaluddin Rumi, "Love Is Reckless," in *The Rumi Collection: An Anthology of Translations of Mevlana Jalluddin Rumi*, ed. Kabir Helminski (Boston: Shambhala Publications, 2005).

CHAPTER 7: A NEW KIND OF POWER

1. For an in-depth study on the anti-imperial message of Jesus and the early church, read John Dominic Crossan, *Render unto Caesar: The Struggle over Christ and Culture in the New Testament* (New York: HarperOne, 2022).

2. R. Alan Streett, *Caesar and the Sacrament: Baptism; A Rite of Resistance* (Eugene, OR: Cascade Books, 2018), chap. 1, pt. 1, Kindle.

3. Hector Scerri, "The Christian Agape Meal: A Manifestation of *Koinonia* and *Diakonia;* The Contribution of Adalbert-Gautier Hamman," *Melita Theologica* 62 (2012): 55–71, https://core.ac.uk/download/pdf/46601909.pdf.

4. "Dum Diversas," *Doctrine of Discovery* (blog), July 23, 2018, doctrineofdiscovery.org/dum-diversas/.

5. Every reader of this book must read Mark Charles and Soong-Chan Rah's book, *Unsettling Truths: The Ongoing, Dehumanizing Legacy of the Doctrine of Discovery* (Downers Grove, IL: InterVarsity Press, 2019).

6. The First Amendment to the US Constitution.

7. I talk extensively about practically cultivating an inclusive community in my book *True Inclusion: Creating Communities of Radical Embrace* (St. Louis: Chalice Press, 2017).

CHAPTER 8: FEAR AND TREMBLING

1. The work of René Girard on mimetic theory is profoundly important here. Check out René Girard, *I See Satan Fall like Lightning*, trans. James G. Williams (Maryknoll, NY: Orbis Books, 2001).

2. I am writing in February 2021, and this number comes from the Climate Clock Project available at https://www.climateclock .world.

3. American Teilhard Association, "Teilhard's Quotes," quoting Pierre Teilhard de Chardin, letter, September 5, 1919, from *Making of a Mind: Letters from a Soldier-Priest 1914–1919* (New York: Harper & Row, 1965), 306, http://teilharddechardin .org/index.php/teilhards-quotes.

RECOMMENDED RESOURCES

Bourgeault, Cynthia. *The Wisdom Jesus: Transforming Heart and Mind—A New Perspective on Christ and His Message.* Boston: New Seeds Books, 2008.

Charles, Mark, and Soong-Chan Rah. *Unsettling Truths: The Ongoing, Dehumanizing Legacy of the Doctrine of Discovery.* Downers Grove, IL: InterVarsity Press, 2019.

Church of the Saviour. https://inwardoutward.org. This community in Washington, DC, has been embodying the subversive love of Jesus for more than sixty years. Their model is one that should be explored by *every* Christian faith community.

Contemplative Resource Center, University of Colorado Boulder. https://www.colorado.edu/center/contemplativeresource/.

Crossan, John Dominic. *Render unto Caesar: The Struggle over Christ and Culture in the New Testament.* New York: HarperOne, 2022.

Delio, Ilia. *Christ in Evolution.* Maryknoll, NY: Orbis Books, 2008.

Eisenstein, Charles. *The More Beautiful World Our Hearts Know Is Possible.* Berkeley, CA: North Atlantic Books, 2013.

Fowler, James W. *Stages of Faith: The Psychology of Human Development and the Quest for Meaning.* New York: HarperCollins, 1995.

Gillette, Carolyn W. "Have the Mind That Was in Jesus." http://www.carolynshymns.com/have_the_mind _that_was_in_jesus.html. A modern setting of the Kenosis Hymn.

Hendricks, Obery M., Jr. *The Politics of Jesus: Rediscovering the True Revolutionary Nature of the Teachings of Jesus and How They Have Been Corrupted.* New York: Doubleday, 2006.

James, Jeff. *Giving Up Whiteness: One Man's Journey.* Minneapolis: Broadleaf Books, 2020.

Joshi, Khyati Y. *White Christian Privilege: The Illusion of Religious Equality in America.* New York: New York University Press, 2020.

Keegan, Robert. *The Evolving Self: Problem and Process in Human Development.* Cambridge, MA: Harvard University Press, 1982.

Kendi, Ibram X. *How to Be an Antiracist.* New York: One World, 2019.

Kivel, Paul. *Living in the Shadow of the Cross: Understanding and Resisting the Power and Privilege of Christian Hegemony.* Gabriola Island, BC: New Society Publishers, 2013.

Kolbert, Elizabeth. *The Sixth Extinction: An Unnatural History.* New York: Henry Holt, 2014.

Presbyterian Church (U.S.A.). "Facing Racism: A Vision of the Intercultural Community Churchwide Antiracism Policy." https://facing-racism.pcusa.org. A collection of resources to facilitate learning about and acting for racial justice.

Rieger, Joerg. *Jesus vs. Caesar: For People Tired of Serving the Wrong God*. Nashville: Abingdon Press, 2018.

Rohr, Richard, and Andreas Ebert. *The Enneagram: A Christian Perspective*. New York: Crossroad, 2001.

United Church of Christ. "White Privilege: Let's Talk." http://privilege.uccpages.org. A curriculum to cultivate conversations about race.

Young, Wm. Paul. *Lies We Believe about God*. New York: Atria Books, 2017.

9 780664 267247